BEEN THERE
AND BACK

BEEN THERE AND BACK

BY FRANK L. WATSON
with Peggy Hoffmann

JOHN F. BLAIR, Publisher
Winston-Salem, North Carolina

PRINTED IN THE UNITED STATES OF AMERICA
BY HERITAGE PRINTERS, INC.
CHARLOTTE, N.C.

Library of Congress Cataloging in Publication Data

Watson, Frank, 1921–
     Been there and back.

     1. Watson, Frank, 1921– 2. Prisoners—North Carolina—
Biography. I. Hoffmann, Margaret Jones, joint author. II.
Title.
HV9468.W36A33   365'.6'0924 [B]   76–49968
ISBN 0–910244–91–X
ISBN 0–910244–92–8 pbk.

For Carolyn

Johnny, David and Lane

Foreword

FRANK WATSON IS ONE OF THE MOST STRAIGHTFORWARD AND DE-
pendable men I know. That may seem a strange thing to say about
a man who has spent most of his adult life either in prison or on
escape. "Frank" was a prophetic name, for it describes him with
uncanny accuracy. He says what he means and there is no doubt
that he will do what he says. In fact it was this very quality, his
dependability, that kept him in frequent trouble and, ultimately,
proved to be the key to keeping him out of trouble.

When the staff of the North Carolina Department of Correction
and I were selecting trainees for the "New Careers in the Treatment of Incorrigibles Project," we deliberately searched for men
who had the respect of the inmate population and had been troublemakers but seemed to be "coming around." Frank filled this
description perfectly. Someone remarked then, "Frank's been a
hell of a problem, but if you can get him to agree to being in your
program, he'll make it. He *always* keeps his word." He was right.

Frank's autobiography is interesting from a number of perspec-
tives. It's a lively adventure story. For the skeptics among you, all
of the incidents he describes are documented in the official record.
Editorial license has been applied only to the names of a few people and occasionally to the wording of conversations, never to their
substance.

This story is also a useful addition to the historical correctional
literature. It is appalling to realize how recently the correctional
systems in this country used such brutal "treatment" as hanging
men by their wrists from rings in the wall.

It is also an important example of a rapidly emerging perspec-
tive in criminological theory—crime prevention through the pro-

vision of positive social roles. Historically the criminal justice system has focused on preventing, deterring, containing, or changing the *negative* behaviors of law violators. Rarely has the system sought to identify and build upon the *positive* behaviors of its unwilling clients. This is a plausible partial explanation of the abysmal failure of correctional programs to "rehabilitate" the inmates with whom they work.

In Frank's case, at least, the correctional system began to realize that the only thing of value to Frank was his honor—his word as "solid con"—and that this could be used to involve him in more constructive behaviors. It was only when they began to deal with Frank on this basis that he began to respond. The last major manifestation of this was his selection for the "New Careers" program. He gave us his word that he would make an honest effort to make a go of it in the project and that he would not use it as a means of trying to escape. Given this commitment, we began to build on his other strengths—his knowledge of the correctional system and its problems and the esteem in which he was held by the rest of the inmate population. He knew if he made it he would have a chance to prove himself in an honest job in the only social system in which he had ever achieved any real measure of success, the prison.

The most important function of this book, however, was its role in Frank's life in prison. It has been in the writing for twenty years or so. Writing his own story was the mechanism Frank used to keep the system from breaking him. It takes a man of extraordinary strength—both physical and emotional—to survive the pressures of the prison. One of his ways of fighting the system was writing about it and the ways he dealt with it. Frank was always a "rebel" as he says. This book, in an important sense, became his "cause."

In short this is the remarkable story of a remarkable man.

CHARLES E. WHEELER, PH.D.

National Institute for Juvenile Justice and Delinquency Prevention

viii

Out of the night that covers me,
  Black as the Pit from pole to pole,
I thank whatever gods may be
  For my unconquerable soul.

In the fell clutch of circumstance
  I have not winced nor cried aloud.
Under the bludgeonings of chance
  My head is bloody, but unbowed.

Beyond this place of wrath and tears
  Looms but the Horror of the shade,
And yet the menace of the years
  Finds, and shall find, me unafraid.

It matters not how strait the gate,
  How charged with punishments the scroll,
I am the master of my fate;
  I am the captain of my soul.

—W. E. HENLEY

BEEN THERE
AND BACK

NORTH CAROLINA / IN THE SUPERIOR COURT
BUNCOMBE COUNTY /
/
IN THE MATTER OF / PROCLAMATION OF
LEWIS FRANK WATSON / OUTLAWRY

WHEREAS, it has been made to appear to the undersigned Judge Presiding at the December, 1956, Term of the Buncombe County Superior Court from affidavits this day filed by A. R. Sluder, Chief of Police of the City of Asheville and A. L. Michael, Chief Deputy Sheriff of Buncombe County, North Carolina, that LEWIS FRANK WATSON is an escaped felon; that the said LEWIS FRANK WATSON was sentenced to a term of five to ten years in State Prison on a charge of breaking and entering and larceny and to a term of ten years in State Prison on a charge of robbery with fire arms; that since his confinement the said LEWIS FRANK WATSON has escaped on two occasions and is now at large presumably in Buncombe County and the City of Asheville:

AND, WHEREAS, it further appears that the said LEWIS FRANK WATSON is now being sought for the crime of escape, a felony, and also for the crime of armed robbery which occurred in Buncombe County on 7 December, 1956;

AND, WHEREAS, it further appears that the said LEWIS FRANK WATSON has openly declared his intention to become an outlaw, having so stated in the Buncombe County Superior Court in February, 1956, and now flees from justice, conceals himself and evades arrest and service of the usual process of the Law:

3

IT IS, THEREUPON, CONSIDERED, ORDERED AND ADJUDGED:

1. That this proclamation of outlawry issue against the said LEWIS FRANK WATSON.

2. That the said LEWIS FRANK WATSON is required forthwith to surrender himself to any Sheriff, or to any other duly authorized person empowered to make arrests, or to any private citizen within the State of North Carolina.

3. That in case the said LEWIS FRANK WATSON fails to surrender himself immediately and continues to stay out, lurk and conceal himself, any citizen of the state may capture, arrest and bring him to justice, and in case of flight or resistance by him, after being called on and warned to surrender, may slay him without accusation or impeachment of any crime.

4. That the Sheriff of Buncombe County, or the Sheriff of any other County in the State of North Carolina in which the said LEWIS FRANK WATSON shall be, be, and he is hereby empowered, and required to take with him such power as he shall think fit and necessary for the going in search and pursuit of, and effectually apprehending, the said LEWIS FRANK WATSON.

5. That this proclamation be published at the door of the Court House of Buncombe County and published in a daily newspaper circulation in Buncombe County for five consecutive days to the end that the said LEWIS FRANK WATSON may be put upon notice that he is subject to be slain if when called upon and warned to surrender he shall fail to do so.

This, the 11th day of December, 1956.

/s/ J. Frank Huskins
Judge of the Superior Court

❋ ❋ ❋ ❋ ❋ ❋ ❋

4

You know the Cookston Hills? Oklahoma? That's where I was born, December, 1921. Sequoyah County, around Muldrow. Has a bad reputation. The James Boys and the Younger Brothers hid out there. Pretty Boy Floyd's kinfolk were from Sallisaw, the county seat. The Dalton Gang used to sneak in there to rest up in the hills after some of their raids.

Sequoyah County butts up against Crawford and Sebastian counties in Arkansas, so a guy on the run could get across a state line pretty easy. The Arkansas River cuts across the county on a diagonal.

Pretty country around there—low hills, woods, the river, game to hunt, good fresh air, rich farm land if you were of a mind to do something about it. The Watsons and the Cooks weren't what you call real dirt farmers, not good ones anyway.

My Grandpa Cook was a preacher, a hell's-fire-and-brimstone Baptist preacher. He and the neighbors had built a little arbor church out in a field. Stout poles held up a roof made of chicken wire filled in with branches. There were rough plank benches with no backs. Grandpa Cook would stand up there in that arbor church pounding away on a homemade plank pulpit, thundering out things about the wages of sin being death—that was one of his favorites—and from what I knew of the folks sitting on those hard benches I figured he had it all wrong. They were as busy sinning as he was preaching against it, but every one of them was hale and hearty.

On Sundays they would come from miles around with horses and wagons or buggies, the women in sunbonnets, the men in patched overalls. There'd be three or four other preachers, but Grandpa could out-holler them all. Then they'd serve huge baskets of fried chicken, yams, deviled eggs, potato salad, green beans, cakes, and pies. I never knew how people could stow away so much food and stay awake for the after-

5

noon's preachin', but they did. Or said they did. I always passed out with my head on Granny's lap. Sometimes I'd wake with a jerk when he'd roar out about preparin' the way for someone fightin' his way through the wilderness and he'd yell out: "He's a-comin'! The time is almost here! We gotta be *ready!* Are ye washed of yer *sins?*"

Once in a while I'd snore in spite of all Grandpa's yelling, and then his temper would fly. I got my name from him. Frank Lewis Watson, not Lewis Frank the way the courts got it. He had some Cherokee blood and a temper like a mad bull. I got that too. So did my mother. That much I remember about her. The shack we lived in, a four-room log cabin back in a meadow, used to rattle at the rooftree when she'd get on my dad and they'd go at it. Maybe that's where I learned to fight, early. I could always fight. Still can, but I try to watch it.

The Cookston Hills would fool you. Looked so quiet and peaceful. Believe me, it was quiet. Nothing for a husky, spunky, fighting kid to do. School once in a while up in the woods in a one-room place with a cast-iron stove and a now-and-then teacher, not always all there. No toys for kids, no playgrounds, swings, teeters, games. No books. I would have read all of them, probably a dozen times. I always liked reading history, especially the Wild West. Plenty happens in history.

Most of the history I heard about was the James Boys. My grandmother knew them. I'd sit on her front porch with her and listen. She had a splinter of wood with blood on it that she kept.

"That's Jesse James's blood right there, Frank. Them dark spots. That's his dyin' blood."

I'd shiver and ask her again, "Where was that, Granny? Here?"

"Up in St. Joe—one o' his own men—gunned him down—in

6

his own house. In '82 that was. When he was dyin', his blood gushed all over. Musta bin a sight to be-hold!"

"Was you there, Granny?"

"I never bin in Missoury. My pappy bought this from a drummer that come through here. Long time ago. They was outlaws, fugitives, all of 'em. Him and his older brother Frank was about as far apart as you and Johnny—three-four years—and they was mighty tough younguns!"

"Was you scared of 'em, Granny?"

She'd laugh and say something about how everyone knew them and how handsome they were. Strong, manly, not afraid of the Devil himself. "Always worried yer Grandpa!" I'd get her started on the Daltons or Ma Barker. Great stories. True ones. I loved every word. I'd dream about the James Boys at night. I could hardly wait for me and Johnny to get bigger.

Then she'd talk about the Hangin' Judge, Isaac Parker, in Fort Smith, Arkansas. "He'd set up a gallows on the street, right downtown. Hardly let the rope cool off. Ol' Judge Parker was a great 'un fer hangin'!"

What I remember best about my father was the real bad beatings he'd give me after he'd come home from a day of job-hunting. This was in the thirties during the Depression. He'd been in the first World War and got himself shell-shocked, so he was real nervous.

But I loved it when he'd let me handle his guns. I grew up loving a gun—later in life it cost me dearly. I was real good with a rifle and pretty fair with a pistol. That pistol fitted right into my hand and was smooth and shiny. I had big strong hands like the rest of me, even as a boy. He was a dead shot and he taught me all he knew.

"If ya aim t'hit, boy, *hit!* Use your eyes! Use your head! Use your hands! Both of 'em. Line it up. Steady! *Now!*" I got a few powder burns, but not for long. "You never heard of them

7

Daltons gettin' powder burns!" he'd holler, and I'd try again. I had to get as good as the Daltons. And the James Boys and all those other great heroes.

Every chance I got I'd go into the woods, sometimes for three or four days at a time. I grew up like an Indian. I loved the forest; the quiet and the beauty would soothe me.

I must have been about five when my father up and left home. I know my brother had been born by then because I had to take care of him, starting when I was three. Some baby-sitter, three years old, but no one seemed to care. He got adopted. He was lucky. I didn't know him or his new folks until I was in my teens. Great folks. He was double lucky.

I was half grown before I saw my father again; he had re-married by then and had four sons. I guess I liked him, but I never really grew to love him. If I had dared love anyone at that time, it would have been my stepmother. He had married a real fine woman. I respected her very much.

My only live hero was my mother's brother, Uncle Jim. He was a messenger on the mail car of a passenger train. He got me a toy pistol just like his, with a holster and belt and all. I'd carry it just like he did his .45. I'd try to walk like him and snap my gun out of that holster for a quick draw. Lucky it was a toy. I'd have killed off half of Sequoyah County and probably not cared either. When he let me play with the real .45, he'd make extra sure it wasn't loaded. I'd go swaggering around with it, and he'd die laughing.

As far as I know I was the only one in the family, either side, that ever got into big trouble, but I made up for all of them. They used to call me the black sheep. Maybe I looked like one: black curly hair, big nose, big shoulders, a disposition more like a billy goat, strong as an ox. Uncle Jim used to say I'd been born fifty years too late.

"You're cut out to be a hell-raiser, Frank. You don't fit in today's world. Them old-time romantic outlaw heroes died out a long time ago. Too much civilization these days for them guys."

We'd both laugh, and I'd say, "Stick 'em up, podner!"

The truth was that I didn't belong anywhere. Not at school, not at home—if you could call it a home, not at Granny's; maybe on the streets, like my mother.

I had a stepfather for a while. That was when the Depression hit. We got a place in Fort Smith, about thirty-eight miles from Grandpa Cook's. I was shaking like a leaf, looking down every street for Judge Parker's Hangin' Gallows, but no luck. We were in a tough neighborhood. That's where I really learned to fight. Three or four kids would waylay me on the way to or from school. I'd fight until I had to stop for breath; then I'd go back for more. I was never a quitter.

One of those boys was later given the electric chair for killing a man in a robbery. He was named Eldon Chitwood. Eldon taught me what it was to be really tough because he knew all the angles. When I got so I could lick him, I thought I was king. He taught me to steal too. I had damn good training, young.

My stepfather was always looking for work. He'd pick up a little here, a little there, but if we didn't steal we couldn't make it. Eldon and I and some of the other kids would wait until the truck farmer came along in his wagon; then while he was at the back door trying to sell something, we'd jump on the wagon and steal everything we could haul off.

"Watch it! He's a-comin'!" We'd jump down and run for dear life. He might chase us but he never caught us.

Depression or no Depression, we had a pretty good diet because we'd have fresh fruit and vegetables from him and from the neighbors' gardens, which I raided all the time; then when it was dark the grownups would go out and steal chickens, a

9

duck, or anything they could lay their hands on. Nobody seemed to think there was anything wrong in it. We had to eat.

There was another divorce, so the Welfare got me and stuck me in the Rosalee Tilles Home for Children—a place for leftover, unwanted kids. I must have stayed there eight or nine years. The food was pretty good but I was always hungry. I was born hungry and never got over it. The big boys got us smaller ones to raid the storeroom and steal oranges and apples. It was locked, but there was a small hole near the ceiling that the manager didn't seem to know about, and the skinnier kids could squeeze through it.

The big boys liked to get the younger ones to fight so they could watch. If we didn't do it, they'd hold us and whip us with a belt. A leather belt. Sometimes I'd get so blind mad I'd fight the big boys too. Pretty soon they all knew who I was and that I had a damn ungodly temper, like a lighted fuse.

We made boxing gloves out of raincoat rubber stuffed with rags. When you got hit with one of those, the blood would fly and you couldn't see straight for the rest of the day.

I always liked to read but I never did like school. When I was about ten, I ran away and got to Grandpa Cook's house. I sat down on the front porch and looked across the hills and started dreaming about Granny telling me stories. Outlaws! Fugitives! Incorrigibles! I couldn't even pronounce the word then, but it had a strong, wonderful sound, like marching music. In-corrigible!

She came out and found me sitting there, a contented little boy who had found his way home. I was hoping she'd bring me corn bread and milk. She made corn bread fit for angels. She swept out the door and didn't even say hello.

"Frank Watson, you done run away agin! How many times is this?"

"I'd rather stay here with you, Granny! Please?"

"Well, son, you can stay as long as you want."

I didn't ever get enough of Granny's corn bread. I'd eat until I'd almost burst, then ask for some more. She always laughed about it. Then the Sheriff came and got me and took me back to Rosalee Tilles.

Three or four of us boys would steal some bicycles and be gone from the orphanage for a week or two, living off the land and carrying on. Then they'd find us and beat us half to death. I ran away every chance I got, so I saw a lot of Arkansas when I was in that orphanage. I got a lot of beatings too, believe me, but a tough kid like me gets used to beatings.

My mother lived someplace nearby, but never came to see me. I sneaked out a couple of times to see her, but then she went to California and I never heard any more of her. I suppose she's dead by now.

The orphanage got the idea of farming us out to work in the fields. Those farmers would work the be-Jesus out of us. Didn't matter whether we were sick in bed or had a broken leg or pneumonia. I got ptomaine poisoning—never was so sick in my whole life—but that farmer made me work anyway, out in the hot sun hoeing beans. I'd have to run the plow, and I was so little I'd have to reach up to hold the plow handles. I'd rake and weed and dig and plant. If I didn't work, he'd lick me, so I worked. Then I ran. I must have been about eleven.

After they caught me and I finally got well, they sent me to a farm owned by an old lady about seventy, the size of a robin and hateful as they come.

"I don't see why ya allus got t'be eatin," she'd whine at me. "I hardly eat a bite all day. I'm strong as a mule!"

"Gitcha one o' them mules 'n' see how *they'd* do without food!" I'd yell back at her. "I'm starved! I gotta *eat!* I can't work this hard without nuthin' in m'belly!"

"Don't ya know they's a Depression on? Who you think you are, Franklin D. Rooseyvelt?"

"He don' do no plowin'!"

So I ran again, while I still could without fainting dead away from hunger.

That's when I found my brother. I didn't even know what his name was. Not Watson. First thing I knew the Welfare decided they'd try me with the people who'd adopted Johnny. They were farmers too, but of a different stripe. I couldn't believe they were so nice. Gave me a clean bed, told me I could have seconds on anything as long as it lasted, bought me a decent pair of shoes and a new shirt. Blue, it was. My brother was turning out great. I wish they'd taken me when I was little. He was damn lucky.

"Call us Mother and Daddy," they were always asking. "We could be your parents, just like we're Johnny's parents."

"I'll try . . . someday." But I couldn't. How could they care anything about me? They were just pretending. And I didn't dare let myself care for them. I was having to look out for *me*. That was all I could handle. I'd been fooled too many times.

I worked there with Johnny and his folks all summer. When I got back to the orphanage, trouble began as soon as school did. One of the teachers hit a boy across the knuckles with a heavy ruler. *Smack!* You could hear the crack clear out at the road. The room got quiet as a graveyard.

I saw red. I picked up the nearest book and let fly with it. It hit her square across the back of her head, and down she went like a poled ox. When she came to and they finally decided that she'd live, they beat me and turned me out, permanently. I was not quite sixteen.

I don't generally hurt women. She was one of the first. I didn't enjoy it, but she deserved it and I'd do it again.

I was beginning to learn about Fugitives. It would be some time before I'd really learn the word Incorrigible.

2

I DON'T KNOW WHY JOHNNY'S FOLKS TOOK ME BACK AFTER THAT but they did. Me and him went to school for a while at Midland, Arkansas, but I hated it so much and made so much trouble that they let me quit. Good riddance. All I was doing was fighting and stirring things up.

When there wasn't any work on the farm, I'd take a rifle and the dog and off we'd go to the woods to roam around for maybe a week. I was what you'd call a loner. I like people well enough, I guess, but I don't like crowds. Even when I'd get asked to a party where there might be some pretty girls and some good eats, I wouldn't go. I might even say I would, then not show up.

They let me stay there a couple of years. I still couldn't call them Mother and Daddy—it sounded silly—but they treated me the same as they treated Johnny and I did all right. Well, some of the boys that worked at other farms around there got to stealing mail from the farmers' boxes. Johnny didn't much want to try it, but I talked him into it. This was near Christmas in 1937.

It was easy enough. We had a couple of horses we rode all the time, and it was about two miles to the mailbox anyway, so we went off like always with no one the wiser. There was a big box of candy and fruitcake sitting in one of the boxes, so we opened it and ate all of it and threw the box away. Best stuff I ever tasted.

One of the other boys tipped me off that the Feds were looking for us, so I ran away. It took them five months to catch up with me. The Welfare people got hold of me and stuck me in the county home for old people. I got scarlet fever, and they kept me in a basement room because it was cooler there. I was clear out of my head for two or three weeks. When I got up I had to learn to walk again—made it easier to catch me; I couldn't run.

It wasn't the first time the law had gotten after me, but it was the first time they really did me in. They wanted to get all the rest of the guys too. When they found out I had a .38 pistol I had stolen from one of the neighbors, they threatened me with all kinds of things, but I didn't rat on anyone and they sent me up for five years. The U.S. Marshals came and got me at Fort Smith and took me to Washington, D.C., showed me the sights, and dropped me off at the Federal reform school, the National Training School for Boys, a place they run like the Army.

They made us go to church there, but I don't remember anything about it except how hard the seats were. And there was never a big meal of home-fried chicken and corn bread afterwards, like I had at Granny's.

I got to be pretty good at football and boxing while I was in D.C. The coach must have seen how good I was, so he took me in and taught me to fight scientifically instead of plowing into every jaw that got in my way. I already knew pretty well how to defend myself, but that guy taught me a lot of extra tricks. I should have thanked him. Maybe he'll read this.

In two years I got paroled, and the bailiff of the court at Fort Smith took me in. He had a son about my age; we got along real good until he started riding me about being a jailbird.

"How's it feel not to have bars in front of those pretty brown eyes, jailbird? Did they call you by your name, or were you just a number? A big number or a little number?" My Cherokee temper boiled up. My parole officer thought maybe Johnny's folks would be big-hearted enough to take me in again. I certainly had to go somewhere.

When I got there, they were in pretty bad shape, barely able to get enough to eat, so I went into town and hunted up my dad. He seemed like an all-right guy and his wife was real nice to me, but they had so many kids—my half-brothers —that I took off again. That was in 1939, no work but W.P.A., and no one would hire a kid when so many family men needed the work. I had a prison record already but I never mentioned that.

An uncle lived out near the river, so I hit him up for a place to stay and he said O.K. He was about sixty. His wife was twenty-two and stacked like a movie star. I didn't know too much about women then, but that girl taught me. Man, what I learned from her! And fast! My face burns yet when I think about it. First time in my life I ever knew what shame meant.

She kept pushing herself at me, but I stayed away from her. After all, I guess you could call her my aunt because she was married to my uncle. And he'd taken me in. Finally she got her girl friend to work on me.

"The house will be empty tonight, Frank," she said, her eyebrows fluttering around. "And the ol' man will be down t'the river, playin' poker and drinkin'. Never comes home till daylight, 'less he's losin'. He don't lose very often. Not him."

I just looked at her, pretending I was stupid. "You'd be a fool, Frank, if you didn't—" Then my aunt came in, looking real sugary, and did the same stuff with her eyebrows. "Nine o'clock O.K., Frank boy?" I tried to turn away but she flung her arms around me, and well—

I was with her near-bout all night, but when the old man came in I was sound asleep in my bed in the loft, flat out done in. I don't know about her. I guess she could have gone on for a week, but I was just a beginner. And she kept after me every chance she got.

Then her sister came to live with them, stacked even better. She was my age. I got out fast. One woman on you is bad enough, but two is a nightmare. And my uncle wasn't exactly blind. I got scared that he'd say something, then I'd say something, and my temper would pop off and I might hurt him. So I made a good excuse about my dad needing me and I cleared out, staying at my dad's at night and spending my days on the river.

There was a hobo jungle on the river's edge. You don't see so many any more, but during the Depression and before World War II got wound up there were hundreds of them. You could meet every kind of person you can imagine, mostly men wanted by the law. They'd give us boys money to get them food, clothes, anything else they needed, so we always had a little pocket change. There were usually four or five women living with them. Sometimes we'd practice shooting their pistols—they all had pistols. A couple were real beauties—stolen, of course. One man had a machine gun. God knows where he got it, but he hung on to that thing like a kid with a toy.

"Couldn't we just shoot one round? Or blanks?"

"No. No one shoots this but me, kid!"

"Why not? We wouldn't hurt anything with it."

"Nope. Makes too much noise. We'd have the law down here."

"You're afraid we'd steal it, that's why."

"Could be. Get your own guns. I ain't running no gunshop!"

So we did. The guns came in handy for holding up stores around Fort Smith, but we never did get much money. There wasn't any in 1939, there or anyplace else. We got shot at a couple of times but never bad hurt. It was a great life, just dangerous enough to be fun. But the police got to nosing around too much, so I went off and joined the Army without telling my parole officer.

They needed big husky kids that could lick their weight in wildcats, so I didn't have any trouble getting in. Didn't mention my prison record. I joined the 10th Combat Engineers Division at Seattle, Washington. I was getting to see a lot of the country. Man, it's a big one!

It wasn't bad doing garrison duty at Fort Lawton, but field duty was a different bag of worms. We built bridges, tank traps, and roads. The sun and that hot wind beat down on us day and night. Sand and dust got in our eyes. When it wasn't the weather, it was a sergeant. If one got too rough with me, I'd wait until I caught him in town off duty, and then I'd beat the tar out of him. The worst was when we'd be on maneuvers and we'd be stuck out there without any chance to get the one that had worked us over.

I started drinking. Seems funny now that I had to be eighteen years old, going on nineteen, before I tasted alcohol, but it's true. And women of course. My aunt had given me a damn good start, and I was already a Pro. Between drinking, wenching, and gambling, I was a mighty busy young man. Even then I tried to keep in shape. Any kind of sport that showed up, I went for it. I was young and strong as a bull, and most of the time I was ready for anything.

They sent us down to California on bivouac, at the Hearst Ranch near King City. It was a rugged life—sleep in pup tents, sleeping bags if you were lucky. If you didn't shake out your bedding or pound it with a rifle, like as not you'd have a rattlesnake for a bedmate.

Some kind of spider—not a snake, thank God—bit me right over the eye, and my head started swelling up until I looked like a red cabbage. They sent me to a hospital in Monterey,

17

where a medic stuck me in hot packs for a week while I was moaning and carrying on, half out of my mind with the pain. It never got any better and I was like a lion with a sore paw. One day they came in and propped me up in what looked like a barber chair.

"Now, Watson," the doc said, with a nasty look on his face because he knew I didn't dare hit him, "you gotta take this straight. Too close to the eye. Can't give you anything to knock you out. Won't take but a minute."

"*What* won't take but a minute? Only takes a minute to die, too!"

There was a starchy nurse and a half-dozen guys in white coats, so I tried to be decent and I asked them, "Well, you could at least tell me, what's going on? If I have to take it straight, I ought to—"

Right then the guy slashed into me with a knife right above my eye. Blood and pus and guck squirted out all over the place, hit him on his pretty white coat. I liked to have shit. Then they stuffed some aspirin and junk into me, told me to simmer down, everything was fine and all that trash.

By the time they turned me loose from that hell-hole and let me get back to my company, I was more than ready for a pass into town, but no go. So a bunch of us went over the hill, me with a bandage across my eye so I looked like a pirate. I felt like one too. I wish I'd had a cutlass. And who should we see but the Company Commander? When we got back to camp, he busted all of us back to Private. I was only a PFC, so I didn't have far to go.

I did better a couple of weeks later when we ran into a carnival. There was a boxer, and they'd pay you so much a round to get in and mix it up with him. I'd just seen a news-reel where Joe Louis whipped Bill Conn, so I jumped up and volunteered.

"Don't do it, so'jer! He'll kill you! Stay outa there, you!"

People were yelling at me from the crowd, but that kind of talk just sets me off. We needed the money, too, to have some fun with at the carnival.

"Don't do it, fella! That guy's dangerous! He'll kill ya!" They kept hollering until there was a nice crowd around to watch us. I didn't pay any attention, just climbed into the ring and started in on him. I'd rush him, hit him, and then hang on to him like a tiger. I got a black eye and a busted lip, but man, that money came in handy. We had a great time with it.

That boxer was so mad I thought he'd explode. He followed me out of the ring and on outside, but someone got hold of him and kept him from jumping me again. He would have had his ass kicked off because a couple of my buddies were with me and we'd have let him have it. We just laughed at him and took off.

When we got back to Fort Lewis from California, a near tragedy happened. We put up our camp on American Lake. They had us build a tower with nets so we could practice boarding ships. Well, we were eating lunch one day and not paying any attention to the tower when a young looie brought in a company of infantry, saw the tower, and decided it was a great place for his men to practice boarding ships. All built and ready for him.

The tower wasn't anchored down, but the half-assed idiot didn't know that and he didn't ask anyone anything about it. He sent his company scrambling up those nets with full field packs, rifles, machine guns. About half his men were on top of that flimsy tower when it turned over with a great *splash!*

I hope to God I never hear a sound like that again. Men screaming, the tower groaning and squeaking and splintering as it fell apart, the horrible waterspout going up as tons and tons of men and gear fell into the water.

We were too far away to see it, but we could hear it clear to the mess tent. Someone came running and yelling to tell us what had happened, and we got there on the double and started diving. By that time, there wasn't anything to see but water and a bunch of heads bobbing up and down on top of it. Some frantic guys on shore tore off their clothes, throwing things every which way so they could start jumping in and trying to save their buddies. The wooden bones of that tower stood up like a kid's set of jackstraws. They started dragging those poor, scared, half-drowned kids out of there, stretching them out on the ground, going in for some more, counting up to see if they had everyone. They were all about the same age as me.

No one died that day because there were so many of us there to pull them out fast, but it was close enough. They had to call in professional divers finally to get the weapons off the bottom. That lake is very, very deep.

3

I HADN'T HAD ANYTHING TO DO WITH THAT TOWER FALLING INTO the lake and nearly killing all those young soldiers, but it scared the pants off me so much that it began to seem as if everything was going haywire. The Army had built a beer hall at one side of the lake, out over the water, with slot machines and all that stuff. It was about a mile from our camp, so at night we'd go there and drink and get into fights with other outfits and have a hell of a good time.

There weren't any M.P.'s there at first, but we tore the place apart so regularly that they began sending four or five at once. In one fight I got hit so hard that I went right through a window, glass and all, and on into that freezing cold lake. I liked to've drowned before they got me out. I never was a good swimmer—probably because I never had a good place to practice. The Arkansas River isn't much for a swimming place. Boxing, football, wrestling, handball—that was my bag. Nothing involved with the water, but everything else in sports.

So the old CO would look us in the eye and snarl, "All right, wise guys. I heard about your performance at the beer hall last night. If you're that full of pizazz, we'll use up some of it with a nice long hike. Full field pack and rifle. Maybe that'll take some of the fight out of you."

He was right. It did for a while. Then one night someone found the company strong box with all the Canteen books in it and broke it open. By then I knew I wasn't the only guy in the company with a record. They ran a check and found out

I was on parole, although I had nothing to do with robbing that strong box. Honest to God I didn't. They thought I did, but they couldn't prove a thing. I got out of that, barely, but it wasn't long until the heat caught up with me again.

There was a girl in Dalton, Oklahoma, who kept bugging me to send her a picture, so I got all duded up in my uniform and had a real jazzy pose taken at the post photo shop. I ordered a real big one so she'd be satisfied. One night—this was in 1940—we were all beering-up at the hall, and we were all pretty drunk when I got the idea of going over there to see if the picture was ready. The man and woman who ran the place were just going out to eat but said they'd be right back.

So I went to the beer hall and had some more to drink.

"Hey, Watson, where's ya pitcher? Less see that han'sum pitcher of the beeeg man from ArKANsas! Where's ya pitcha, so'jer boy?"

"Ain't ready."

"Whaddaya mean, ain't ready? Why doesn't our noble HEro go and *make* it ready? Huh? *Why?*"

The old Cherokee temper began boiling up, so I got myself right back to that photo shop. It was closed. I waited around for a while but they didn't come back, so I kicked the door in.

I went on in and started looking around for my picture. The place wasn't very big.

"What's going on here? Who are you? What are you doing in here?"

I heard a man and a woman behind me, and I tried to turn around and tell them I was just looking for my picture, but I was too drunk to know which way to look for them. Their voices seemed to be coming from all corners of the room. There was a cash box under the counter with $400 in it, but I hadn't touched it. The man started cursing, and the woman went tearing off to call the M.P. Funny, they didn't seem to

22

be afraid of me, just mad. The M.P. came roaring in and grabbed me.

So it was the guardhouse for six months. And there was a riot, so they put me on bread-and-water for ten days. I lost weight like mad and got myself into a mean temper. They gave me and some other guys the job of policing officers' row and the PX—picking up trash, that is. When we'd pick up stuff behind the PX, the guard would watch for us while we would steal cases of beer and cigarettes, chocolate bars, anything we wanted. The guard always got his cut, and it worked out fine. Once I got careless and took the M.P.'s club away from him and got into one hell of a fight with him. I sure paid for that.

Court-martial for Frank Watson. Off parole, trouble in the guardhouse, breaking into the photo shop—the list got pretty long. *Dishonorable Discharge.*

The U.S. Marshal came and got me and took me to Englewood, Colorado, to finish up the five-year sentence they'd paroled me on.

Man, that was the place, Englewood. They had gangs there. Bad gangs. When I arrived, I sized up the situation and took over one of the gangs. I knew I had to. When some of the guys we knew were finks from another gang went to the PX to get something, I'd send one of my gang to take it from him. If he squealed to the guard, we'd beat him up in the night. Throw a bedsheet over his head, then beat the be-Jesus out of him with a padlock wrapped up in a sock. When we got tired of that, we'd roll him in the sheet and tie him up on the bar, where the guard would find him when he came around to make the count.

The middleweight champion of California showed up there at Englewood, so I took him on. We fought in the toilet. I stayed with him the whole way. He didn't make me quit, but

I got the worst of it. That's what these scars are under my left eye.

They put me in the hole for fighting. Maybe I should spell out what the hole, the segregation cell, is. The hole is usually a room about seven feet long, four feet wide, with no windows, no light, no toilet, no washbasin, only a slit through the door so the guard, the screws or jacks we called them, can see you. You had to shit in a tin can, and that damn can would stay in with you maybe four or five days until some screw, sick of smelling it out in the hall, would come and empty it so you could start over.

You had no bedding, but slept on the cement floor naked, winter and summer. Once in a while a prison might have a hole that was a little better. Sometimes they were worse. In the winter the floor could be covered with ice. It makes me laugh when prisoners today squawk to the Governor about being denied TV or having someone check their mail.

Once at Englewood I caught a fink ratting on me to the guard. I walked up and smacked him in the jaw.

"Why in hell'd you do that, Watson?"

"I hate a rat!" I told him as simple as I could so he'd understand it.

Four guards locked my arms behind me, and when we got to the mess hall door, they opened the door with my head. There was a lot of snow in Colorado that winter. A lot. And it was cold. The hole was deadly, but man, I decided to survive.

About that time the Japanese bombed Pearl Harbor, 1941. They let out a lot of guys so they could go into the Army, but not me.

"Watson, you're a guy that can't take orders!"

"Yeah? But I can shoot, anything that's got a bullet in it. Damned sight better'n you fat-asses."

"Takes more than that to make soldiers. No go."

"I'll get into it, one way or another. Just you watch."

So me and five other guys made up a blackjack and a knife for each man. We had a tool to take the lock off the outside door. It was snowing hard, so we figured the guard on the tower wouldn't be able to see us so good, and some of the other screws, off-duty, were loafing in the day room. Saturdays and Sundays a lot of them sat in there reading movie magazines, joke books, and *Popular Mechanics.*

When the guard on duty came around to take the count, we planned that we'd grab him, tie him up, take the lock off the door, go up over the buildings and down and over the double fence. There was always the chance that the guards could get a shot at us, but with all that snow they wouldn't have too good an aim.

We had everything ready. It was only five minutes until we were to start out. All of a sudden twenty guards with shotguns and machine guns and rifles came in on us, grabbed us all and put us on lockup.

Who ratted?

The guy that used to be the leader of my gang before I took it over was supposed to be going with us. Later I found out that he had put the finger on us after he lost his nerve. There we were, the whole crowd of us, stuck in solitary because he had no guts. I sent word that he'd better not be there or any place near there when I got out. I didn't know then that none of us were getting out. None. When the warden came around to talk to me about the break and the plans we had made, he was damn serious.

"Watson, I'll level with you. If you don't get your head screwed on pretty fast, you're going to end up in the electric chair."

I sat there and looked at him, not saying a word. *It'll be a damn sight warmer there than it is here*, I wanted to say. I felt real mean inside. I was so mad, but he was mad too and something told me to hold it in.

"Just to help you remember what I said, Watson, I'll send you somewhere that you can't get away from, and you'd better not try it. They'll know how to take care of you if you do."

So they moved me. Leavenworth, Kansas. I was twenty.

I got to know the inside of the hole at Leavenworth better than my own cell. I got sent in regularly for fighting other men or even the guards. One of the men in the hole was Robert Stroud, later known as the Bird Man of Alcatraz.

After a while they let me work in the powerhouse as a pipe fitter. I stayed there until March, 1944, when I finally got out after I had done every day of that five-year spot for stealing one lousy box of fruitcake and candy from a mailbox. The war had been going on for two and a half years. There were plenty of changes while I was in prison, but I guess there wasn't any change in me. Unless it was for the worse.

They gave me ten dollars and a train ticket to a burg in Arkansas called Bauxite, just outside Little Rock. There was a mine where they get bauxite. I think they make aluminum out of it. It was in the air so thick you couldn't breathe without filling your lungs with bauxite. I didn't stay long. Me and a couple of the brothers got fed up, so we lit out and ended up in the swamp country. I got malaria. God, but I was sick. As bad as that dose of ptomaine. Worse, really.

There were a couple of girls who made life easier for me— all those months with no women—but it wasn't long before they got after me too hard, so I just took off one day and never went back.

I'd been locked up in Leavenworth for a year and a half, but I'd held off from the girlboy stuff that went on, maybe because I knew I'd be getting out. But for guys sent up for twenty or thirty years—well, what else is there? The girlboy is as common in prison as breathing.

The Star Amusement Shows were playing in Judsonia, Arkansas, and I got myself a job as a boxer. I'd get on the platform in boxing trunks, show off my Charles Atlas figure, and challenge anyone in the crowd. The worst part of that was the home towners. If I'd beat up one of their boys, they'd pull knives and try to take the tent apart with me in it. All you had to do was yell, "Hey, Rube!" and the fun would start.

Then the girls would come around and give me the eye, but that wasn't always too good. I might have to fight the whole family. Or a girl would try to get me to beat up her boy friend because he was too cocky and needed trimming down a notch. A lot of fine girls around there in Arkansas, real fine little girls. With plenty of what it takes.

I don't know what made me think I could swim across the river at a little town called Black Rock there in Arkansas. It was about a half mile wide with a strong current in the middle. When I got out there, I finally had to admit that I wasn't going to make it. I tried to turn around or push harder or do anything to get me headed toward dry land, but I got a cramp in my leg. I started yelling, "Help! Help!" One of the boys from the carnival heard me and swam out. I put my hands on his shoulders, and he got me back on to the bank. If I'd lost my head and not done what he said, I'd have been a goner.

I guess it was the first time in my life that I took orders from anyone. I lay there on the bank, panting, trying to thank the guy, but mostly wondering why I'd been so lucky. A carnival boxer, jailbird, thrown-away orphan must have been needed someplace in the world, or he'd have gone under. That mood didn't last long—I've practically forgotten it.

That same night at the carnival I fought a couple of local blowhards and won. I was in great shape in spite of that close squeak, so of course the draft board heard about it and sent word that I should come in for a physical examination. I probably sounded exactly like what their Army needed, but I told them the kind of discharge I had and that turned them off. I wish I'd lied to them and gone back into the Army. I sure did want to get back in. I might have made a real good soldier. They were desperate for men, too.

Instead, I must have fought a hundred guys at the carnival. I got to be so good that the owner of the show would offer a hundred dollars to anyone who could stay beyond the first round. He knew his money was safe; I usually knocked them out in a couple of minutes.

The war was still on and I wasn't in it. They were drafting fathers of young children, guys with flat feet, poor eyes, almost any kind of male body under eighty, but they didn't want Frank Watson, six feet tall, weight one hundred sixty-five pounds and all muscle, unencumbered with even a pet cat, twenty-two years old and full of beans. Frank Watson, tiger, ex-con, ex-PFC, a free man now with exactly $13.41 in his pockets, very bitter toward life and living.

I had done five years in prison for stealing one fruitcake and a mess of chocolate fudge.

4

I ONCE WRESTLED THE JUNIOR HEAVYWEIGHT OF ARKANSAS. IT was just for show, but most of the other fights were for blood. I was only a middleweight then, about 165 pounds, but I fought some men that weighed over two hundred. I fought all over Arkansas and won every time.

When the show went into winter quarters, I went back to Fort Smith to stay with my dad and drive a transfer truck. It came out in the paper that they were recruiting men to go overseas on a construction job for the U.S. Corps of Engineers. It would be at Santa Maria Island in the Azores, owned by Portugal, building an airfield for planes to stop and refuel on the way from Europe to the United States. If the Army wouldn't have me, I could at least help someplace.

First they sent us to Little Rock for shots, then to Kansas City for the paper work and passports, six hundred of us. After that nothing happened. We stayed so long in KC that our money ran out. We ran loose, sleeping wherever we could, picking up any old job for a few bucks.

The construction company tried to find day jobs for us. Some of the office girls slipped us eating money when they could. If you could stand the pace, you could sleep with a different broad every night, but that soon got old. We tried sleeping in the train station, but the railroad police ran us out. One of our guys stole a suitcase and found in it a brand new Colt .38.

He let me have it for thirty bucks and said he'd wait for his money until I pulled a job. A friend and I pulled several small jobs, got anywhere from $150 to $300, enough to keep us alive at any rate. The police were running crazy. They were as glad as we were when we were finally shipped out of town.

Another three weeks at a camp in Virginia, waiting for passports. The F.B.I. managed to pick up a couple of guys trying to sneak out of the country, but they didn't have anything on me, so I got on the ship, headed east.

Boy, was I seasick! I'd try to sleep on deck if the weather wasn't too bad. Good fresh salt air. Below deck was bad. *Stank.* Everybody throwing up all over the place. Me too. A Pro boxer and I put on a couple of half-hearted shows to take the men's minds off being seasick. None of us got over it until the damn boat docked; then we were O.K. in two minutes.

"Man, oh man, we can get in some swimming!" Everybody was whooping because they were tickled with the sight of those beautiful beaches.

"Take a look over the side, you bastards! Take a look!"

Sharks! Ten, fifteen feet long. Hungry. *Teeth!* Then didn't they put us on a landing barge with no sides. I got myself square in the middle with everyone jammed in around me like Vienna sausages.

It rained night and day. Cool, wet, miserable. Mud to your knees. I worked on the runway, heavy equipment. Good money. We'd work seven days a week, ten to fifteen hours a day, half of it on the night shift.

Nothing at all to do when we weren't working. I found a girl anyway. Her mother had a lot of land and wanted us to marry. If we did, she'd give it to us. I don't know why I didn't take the old lady up on it.

When you didn't show up for work, they had a stockade. I was in it four times. Funny, when I left the States, I wasn't in any trouble and nobody was looking for me.

They'd put you in for at least thirty days, a damn long time to be away from my girl. I'd sneak out of the line-up and get to the latrine that backed up against the fence; a couple of guys would hoist me over, give me some money, and I'd be gone. I'd stay with my girl for a while, and then I'd get a gunnysack of brandy. A quart was about sixty or seventy cents.

I came in by a gravel pit at the back of the stockade where trucks loaded rock and gravel for the runway. Once when I was easing along, two big flashlights came on me. I could see the guards with pump shotguns.

"All right, Watson. Get your hands up. *Quick!* Outta there!"

I slipped the brandy down into the mud puddle I was standing in; then they put me in the hole. They had a humdinger of a hole there. Back to the stockade in the morning. When the truck drivers came in, I pointed to the stash of brandy, and they pitched it over the fence. Some of the bottles broke. Made a nice smell.

Sometimes we had boxing and wrestling shows for soldiers on their way home from the war zone. Once General Holland M., "Howlin' Mad," Smith was there watching. I was nearly kayoed in the fifth round, but I came from behind and won the match. The General called me over, said I had plenty of guts and I'd make a good Marine. I liked that.

That spring, 1945, I won the heavyweight championship of the Islands. We were a rough lot, and I was one of the roughest.

Three months of bulldozing and mud was enough, so I took off. I had plenty of gook money, *escudos*, so I hid at my girl's house. The M.P.'s shook down the whole village, but I'd climb up on the roof of her two-story house and hide behind the chimney. Dumb asses never thought to look there.

I got braver and went to the PX to pick up a couple of things, but an M.P. saw me before I saw him, drew his .45 on me, yelled for help, and slapped me back in the stockade, a brand new one, tight as a drum, guards at each corner. Then the M.P. captain came around and said they were shipping all the fuck-ups like myself back to the States.

The crummy bastards herded us all to the dock and stayed on the beach until the ship sailed. If it hadn't been for the damn sharks, we'd have all jumped overboard and swum ashore. Every manjack of us was in love, or thought he was.

We tied up for water at San Magill Island, about fifty miles away, and there we got the word that Germany had finally surrendered. Knowing damn well what would happen, the Captain gave orders that no one but the ship's crew was to go ashore.

At dark a bunch of the little native boats—they called them bum boats or bomb boats, but we never did get it just right—came alongside and took some of the men ashore, but a couple hundred of us went over the dock side of the ship. At the town end of the dock, there was a gate with a guard. We hit the gate running, tore it down, ran over the guard, and headed for the bright lights. We all hoped the idea of surrender was catching.

It was. I spent a great night with the wife of the sergeant of police. He worked the night shift. So did I, man! Her mother was getting up trade for her. She was young and pretty. I was young too.

Every guy got back on that ship in time for it to sail. San Magill is a great place to visit, but— We gambled and slept and drank all the way home. The food was good, and I wasn't seasick at all. I won the anchor pool of $250 when we docked at Charleston, South Carolina. Got through Customs fine. I had three diamond watches and other contraband on me. So did everyone else. Nobody got caught.

One of my shipmates invited me to Marietta, Georgia, to his sister's place. That's where I met Betty Sue. She was beautiful. Still is. Fine and sweet as they come. It didn't take us very long to realize we were right for each other. Within three days we were married by a Jaypee in Marietta.

I'd never been so happy. Someone cared for me and wanted to stay with me always. I'd look down at her and blink my eyes. She was eighteen, nicely rounded, dark hair, brown eyes, beautiful. And mine.

We went first to her folks' farm in the mountains of western North Carolina. They thought no one, especially me, was good enough for their precious daughter. They were probably right. Her mother—she was a fine woman, understand—had a terrible temper. A real Cherokee temper, I told her once when mine hit hers head-on. I let her know that by damn no woman was going to boss me around, not without some flack.

She'd try to get at me through Betty Sue, sweet little Betty Sue. "Get Frank to do this. Tell Frank to do that." Then she got tougher. "Make that no-good husband of yours come here and do this."

Betty Sue knew right from the start, but her mother never did, that you don't get Frank to do *anything* by giving him orders. I never laid a hand on her then—I have always respected women, especially older women—but man, I wanted to. I couldn't stay around there, so I got a job logging up in Highlands, N.C. I'd work all week, go home Friday night half-pooped until I got my strength built back up, and there was Betty Sue, waiting. Her mother was waiting too.

You don't log in the winter, so I started cutting right-of-way for a power company, another tough job. When that was over, I went to a place near Knoxville, Tennessee, but my wife wouldn't go with me. She was expecting our baby, and she thought her folks needed her too. I had to pay high rent, eat in hash joints, and get home on weekends. I wasn't ahead one red cent. I'd been going pretty straight all those months, but

33

it wasn't getting me anywhere. And it sure as hell scared me to think about trying to buy food for a baby too. People were always griping that babies cost money every time they draw a breath. They were right. Doctor bills, shoes, clothes. And me hardly coming out even.

The guy that ran the eating place cashed payroll checks every weekend. On Friday night he'd have several thousand dollars on him when he walked home with a couple of waitresses who lived at his house. I got myself a Colt .38, put a woman's stocking over my face, and waited behind the bushes in his front yard.

"Hold it!" I stepped out in front of them. "Hold it right there, all of you! Turn around! Drop the money on the ground!"

"What money?"

"Don't pull that 'What money?' stuff on me! *Drop it!*"

"I ain't got no money! I left the payroll cash over at my brother-in-law's, in his safe. Who in hell are you?"

I cocked my pistol. He could hear it, like a firecracker. "I mean business, mister. Fork it over!" He handed me his wallet, and I frisked all three of them. About a hundred bucks in his billfold, seven or eight between the two girls. His wife heard the racket, opened the door, and quick called the police.

It took me all night to get away from those carloads of cops. A time or two I thought they had me. Next day I went into the hash joint to eat, and the cops had it all staked out. Didn't recognize me. I acted real interested in what they were doing to catch the thief.

I had a couple more close ones, so I headed back to the farm. My little son was born there, a beautiful, dark-haired baby, like Betty Sue. I was afraid to touch him, he was so tiny.

One night, when she was still poorly from having the baby, her brother and I went into town to the movies. When we were leaving, a guy got mad because he said I got between him and his girl. When he swung at me, outside, I turned around and beat hell out of him.

A damn policeman stood there and watched. Said the guy had had it coming for a long time. I got a busted right hand and a black eye for doing what the cop was too scared to do. Maybe I should'a been a cop.

When I got home all banged up, Betty Sue flung at me, "Frank Watson, you ain't nothin' but a bully. An ugly, hell-bent, fightin' bully. Someday you're gonna get yourself killed." And we got into it. Her temper was as bad as her mother's.

I guess her real trouble was that she was so damn religious. Her whole family was religious, and they'd all stick together, the way mountain people do.

Worse yet, Betty Sue had been brought up to think that sex was dirty. I'd damn near have to fight her every time. I love to kiss and pet my women. One morning at breakfast I kissed her on the neck, and she hit me smack in the mouth. Split my lip. Sweet little Betty Sue! So I slapped her. Hard. And she cried and carried on, and I said how sorry I was.

Another time we were having it out in the bedroom, and momma came in and said, "Frank Watson, don't you hit her!" I hadn't been planning to, but I slapped her mother onto the bed and slapped Betty Sue down beside her.

Her daddy came running in with an axe—he'd been chopping firewood—and tried to hit me with it. Could have killed me. I grabbed the axe with my left hand and hit him in the ribs with my right hand and broke three of them.

I hated that. Her daddy was a good man.

I decided that it was time to get out.

5

MAYBE IT WAS A GOOD THING I GOT OUT BECAUSE A GUY IN KING'S Mountain talked me into turning Pro as a boxer. I told him it would take me six months to get in shape for fighting because I hadn't had on a pair of gloves for over a year. He got me a room at a friend's house where there were a woman and her daughter and son, and found a practice gym.

One time I came in to take a bath and get cleaned up, and the woman was sprawled across her bed with the door open. She called for me to come in. I told her I was going into town but I'd be back later that night.

"The kids will be asleep by that time," she said, all smiles. "My son works at the cotton mill, and my daughter's in high school, so they both have to get up early." She gave me a big wink, wiggled around a little, and said, "I'll see you later, tiger. Don't forget!"

"I never forget, doll," I told her, pulling on my pants. "Later!" And I gave her a big wink too.

But that time I forgot. I was going with a girl in town, and she asked me to marry her. She kept me there pretty late, so when I got to my room I fell into bed and went to sleep. The woman came in and woke me up. She wasn't too good. Her pussy was so big from all the traffic that I couldn't get any traction, and she sounded like a wind-blown horse puffing away. I rode her so hard she was plumb worn out before I got going good. She wanted me to marry her, but I told her two or three times I was already married.

Well, she went to work early at the cotton mill, and I was reading the paper in the kitchen when her daughter came in, nothing on but a robe, open all the way, grabbed me around the neck, and started kissing me.

"I know all about you and Momma, Frank, honey," she said. "I want some too." So I gave it to her. She was sixteen, going to high school. After just screwing the old lady, I couldn't get up much interest, but she played and felt and kissed me until I let it all hang out. She had a good tight ass, and I nearly got hooked on it. She wanted us to get married, even though she knew too that I was married and had a son.

Three women in a coupla hours! Well, I've heard that there's a man for every woman, and for a while there, by damn, I began to think it was me.

On the other hand, if you're going to be a Pro fighter, you have to win. And if you're going to win, you can't train on pussy, young or old. My manager laid down the law.

When my first Pro fight came up, I got beat. He couldn't put a glove on me for the first four or five rounds, but then I ran out of steam and he had me. I got a rematch with him and felt sure I could beat him, but he got killed in a barroom where he was drunk and trying to wreck the place. The bartender killed him with a .25 automatic. He was a nice guy and had a beautiful wife and family. I felt bad about it.

You can see how it would be. Trying to fight as a Pro, losing the first go-round. Then with three women after me and a wife and child up in the mountains, it was no go. My daddy was working in Oklahoma City, so I wrote him that I was coming in on the bus and he should meet me. I got a job and wrote to ask Betty Sue to come and bring the baby. She never answered.

I went to New Mexico to operate a bulldozer. When the guys found out I was a fighter, they asked me to give a good licking to the boss. We all hated him because he'd cuss us out, for anything or nothing. We got our checks at the post office, and when he handed me mine I said to him, "I hear you been bad-mouthing me and cussing me behind my back. They say you called me an S.O.B. and a bunch of other things."

"So what if I did?" He outweighed me by more than fifty pounds, but I was young and in good shape. "What you gonna do about it, smart ass?"

"Nobody cusses me, to my face or to my back, bastard!" I hit him on the jaw. He got up from the floor and yelled for the police. I flattened him again. That time he didn't get up but yelled from there.

"Get the cops! This S.O.B. is—"

They hauled us to court, and the judge looked us over. "Seems to me like the young man took on quite a handful," he said, rubbing his chin. "Must be about a fifty-pound handicap there, eh? Ten dollars each. For fighting in the post office."

The boys paid my fine, grinning like crazy. The judge grinned too.

That was the town where I stole and flew an airplane for the first time, maybe the last. I nearly drove it into the town water tank, but the other guy and I finally got it back down on the ground, right side up, and put it back in the hangar. I don't think the owner ever knew.

After whipping the boss, there was nothing left but for me to get out of town anyway. He'd blacklisted me with the oil companies, but I got a railroad job up near Chicago. The camp was dirty—bugs and filth so thick it stank. I stayed a couple of days, watched Tony Zale and Rocky Graziano in training—man, what Pros!—and finally took off for Fort Smith again. I saw a lot of country there for a while.

Some stores got held up and the police started snooping around, so I began drifting, working here and there at a dozen different kinds of jobs, mostly in North Carolina.

Once on a dark, rainy night, I found a safe in an office in Gastonia and took it out to the garage to open it. Only a couple of hundred bucks, so I went back up to King's Mountain. First I had to have a weapon. There was a hardware store that had a big ventilator on the roof, two stories up. I cut my hand getting it open and climbing down through it to a storeroom on the top floor.

Downstairs I got two new Colt .38s, loaded them, found a little money, got two more weapons and ammunition, opened the back door, and took a cab to Gastonia.

Word got to me that my wife's father and brother were laying for me. If I showed up at their farm, they'd shoot me. That was like waving a red flag in front of a bull, so I went to the farm. I got out of the cab and started to open the front door when her brother, who was just out of the Marines and had been on Iwo Jima, came out the door with a rifle.

"Don't come no further, Frank. If you do, I'll kill ya. I ain't foolin'!"

I didn't answer, just kept walking. I reached under my coat, got the .38, and cocked it. The minute the cab driver saw those guns, he took off like a big bird and drove straight to the police.

I turned sideways to my brother-in-law to make a smaller target, and he ran back into the house. Betty Sue came running out, begging me not to shoot.

"Honey, I ain't gonna shoot first." I kept right on walking and went into the house to see my son. He was like a picture in the magazines with dark eyes, curly hair; kind of scared of me, but he let me hold him.

I guess seeing me holding my little boy on my lap and talking sweet stuff to him kind of cooled them off because my wife finally said she'd take me back and we should find someplace else to live. I had to hide all day and get to Gastonia that night.

I knew the cops would be after me, but a couple of my friends that were staying at a hotel there said they'd hide me.

Sure enough, the police found me. They put handcuffs on me, then searched the guy's room. They found the pistol under the mattress, and in a dresser drawer they got my billfold with about fifty bucks in it. One of the bills had the manager's initials on it. They had me.

The judge said he'd go easy on me because I leveled with him. Gave me four-to-ten, then cut it to two before I left the courtroom. The police had told me it might go better if my wife and baby came so the judge might put me on probation out of sympathy for a young mother and her child. She wouldn't do it.

"Say, Watson, how about selling us those two .38s?" one of the cops asked me.

"Sure. If I'm gonna be in jail, I don't have no use for them."

Damn fool. Didn't I know they'd check the numbers? That's the first thing they did and found out they were stolen from the hardware store at King's Mountain.

The trial for that job was in Shelby. The judge seemed to think the whole thing was one great big joke. That teed me off, so I told him off, and that made him mad. He gave me three-to-six years, the time to run concurrently. That point took some argument, but he finally gave in. I was sent to Gastonia to jail, to Raleigh for processing, and to Franklin Prison Camp, Franklin, North Carolina.

They put me in the rock hole there, so I learned to break rock the hard way.

The rock hole was different from the punishment hole. First they blasted a hole out of the side of the mountain, then they put in fifteen or twenty prisoners, under armed guard, with sixteen- or twenty-pound sledgehammers to make little chunks out of the big chunks. The prisoners loaded the rocks onto a dump truck to be hauled to a rock crusher nearby and made into gravel for the North Carolina roads.

The worst thing at the rock hole, except for the forced, hard labor, was the foreman. He had an I.Q. of Minus Zero, and he hated me because I wouldn't speak to him. I'd manage to hit the rock against the grain so the splinters would fly and hit him. They hurt like fire. I'd get hurt too, but I didn't care. The important thing was to get him.

One of the boys tried to run from the rock hole and got hung up on a barbed wire fence at the outer edge. A guard walked up and shot him dead. That's how bad it was. And the foreman had me put in the punishment hole at night. Nothing to eat, just two salt crackers. You had to reach through a hole in the door to get the crackers; then they'd make them break in two.

In the winter, when it rained, water would seep in and there would be ice on the floor. One boy's feet froze, so they had to amputate them.

Up to then I didn't give a hootin' damn what happened to me, but at that rock hole I got so full of hate that if I had bit myself I'd have died of poison in three seconds. I kept telling myself that they'd never break me down like they did some of the guys. Some were starved for so long it ruined their health.

One spring they had to use the rock hole men to clear the roads of landslides. It looked like a good chance to escape. Another guy and I talked it over and made our plans. The road ran through a big pasture, without a tree or bush for five or six hundred yards.

"See that road?" the kid whispered. "Let's hit it!"

The guard was standing about fifteen feet from us, watching. He had a pump gun and a .38. We threw down our bush axes and took off. The guard yelled *Halt!* and fired his shotgun at us. I could hear the buckshot zinging over our heads.

When I looked back, his gun had jammed and he was trying to get another shell into the chamber, so I thumbed my nose at him and leaped another fence. The boy said he knew his way around. We took off our shirts and set fire to them so we could drag them after us to kill the scent. That way the dogs couldn't follow our trail.

We ran and walked and went through creeks and brush, but just about dark, when we thought we had them beat, the boy led us smack into a pack of guards and dogs. They put their guns on us, got the cuffs on us, went to a store and called the camp.

The dog wagon came to get us. The dog wagon is a pickup truck with a barred cage, used for carrying bloodhounds and transferring prisoners all over the state. In the winter you could freeze to death in the dog wagon.

That was the first time I was ever in stripes and chains, 1946. We also got ten days in the hole, then back to the rock hole. The foreman was waiting. He started picking at me again. The more he picked, the worse I acted. I had chains on my legs night and day. The guards checked every few hours to make sure I hadn't found a way to get out of them.

I even had to sleep in chains. There's a way you can get pants on and off over the leg-irons, but it's quite a trick. Roll down your right pants leg, turning it wrong side out as you go. Get your foot out of it, roll it along the chain between your ankles and back up over your left pants leg, still wrong side out. Both legs of the pants will then be on your left leg, the right one on top of the left one. This takes quite a while, but hell, you've got lots of time, like maybe six months or a year. Now, very carefully squeeze both pants legs under the left cuff of the leg irons. Slide them out and they're off.

What happens if you don't learn to do this? You're in the same pants for as long as you're in irons, unless the pants rot off. Three months. Six months. A year?

They used dynamite to shoot the rock down, so we began stealing dynamite and electric caps. They'd shake us down, but they never found mine. Never would have if one of the guys hadn't chickened out because he was afraid I'd blow up everyone in the prison camp. He put the finger on me. Ten more days in the hole without food. Saved them a board bill.

You wouldn't think I'd meet a nice girl at a place like that, but I did. Her son was in with me, and when she came to visit him, she saw me hobbling around in my chains and told him to ask me to write to her. By that time Betty Sue had divorced me and had gotten custody of my boy, not that I blamed her. I'd been a hell of a husband for her. To tell the truth, I'm still fond of her to this day. Betty Sue is one of those things a man doesn't get over.

Anyway, Angie started writing to me every day and coming to see me every visiting Sunday. It was wonderful. The Captain told her to keep it up. If I didn't get a letter every day, I was that much harder to live with and would probably try to leave.

"Frank, honey, don't try to escape. Serve out your time and get away as a free man. You'll get yourself killed sooner or later." She sounded like the warden at Englewood and Betty Sue and— I'd never say to anyone that I didn't much care.

"I'm too tough for them, Angie," I'd say, laughing, and she'd frown and say, "Look who's winning so far, Frank."

"Don't you want us ever to get married?" I'd ask her. "If I'm in here with this damn jewelry on my legs, I ain't much good to a woman."

"Right. But don't run, honey. Please don't run!"

What a nice girl she was. She had to be older than me—I never found out how much—but she was wiry, blonde, little, cute as a bug, and a real tonic for me. She had three kids; the oldest was in the camp with me.

"Angie, I'm gonna tell you one thing straight. Frank Watson is gonna get out of here!"

6

THEY ALWAYS TOOK US TO THE ROCK HOLE IN A TRUCK THAT HAD a top on it. When you got out the back of it, you had to go right past a guard riding in a trailer hooked on behind. Three of us had it fixed to run. The guard always made me sit up close to the cab. When we turned off the highway to the rock hole, I told the guy in the middle to get out of the way. The other two boys were clear at the back. They dropped off easy; then I bent down and slid along the bench toward the door.

The guard had pulled his .38 by then. When I jumped, he shot through the windshield of the trailer at me, four times. The glass cut me over the eye, but without the glass those four shots would have hit me square in the face, and I'd have been killed right there.

When I hit the ground, it flipped me over, with the truck doing thirty-five or forty miles an hour. It stopped as soon as the shooting started. The guard jumped out and gave his shotgun to the foreman to keep the other prisoners from leaving while he chased us. I got to my feet, and we headed down a little side road with the guard at our heels, shooting the .38. One of the shots clipped my hair.

He kept on shooting, one of the bullets singing off the barbed wire fence I was holding apart for the other two. I didn't even look around. The screw talked to the Captain about it later, said I was either crazy or had a lot of nerve.

If he hits me, he hits me, I thought. Why watch for it? Somebody asked me the other day if I'd ever been suicidal, and I just laughed. Then I thought about things like this—a quick death and an easy one—I heard that someplace. Well, I wasn't hunting death. I like to live too much for that.

I had on other clothes under my stripes, so I pulled off the stripes as soon as I got to the woods and away from the screw. We three went puffing and scrambling up to the top of the hill.

"Hey, let's grab some rest!" I told them. "I'm winded."

We were kind of leaning up against some trees when I heard a sound. There was the screw—right behind us with a long-barreled Long Tom shotgun. He had gone by a farmer's house, and the farmer had given him the gun. He had come up a logging trail and cut us off.

"*Halt!* All of you!"

"Halt? *Hell!*" I turned to run. He shot me in the left arm. It knocked me down, and the other two guys came to help. "Keep movin', you damn fools! Git outa here! Git!" They got.

Before I could pull myself up, the guard stuck the gun in my face. When he pulled the trigger, I knew I was done for, but it was a single barrel and he'd forgotten to reload. A bunch of farmers heard all the racket and came running up.

One of them knocked the gun barrel up and took it away, cussing the guard. Probably saved my life. Some guys would have got converted right then.

I must have sat by the rock hole for an hour waiting for the dog wagon, bleeding, boiling mad.

They got me a tetanus shot, stuck on a Band-Aid or two, and tossed me in the hole. Cement floor, no food, my arm swelling up as big as my head. Doc Engel, who came to the camp when they needed him, pulled me through. Pills, shots—I usually steer clear of any kind of medicine, but those saved me. When he saw how bad my arm was, he made them take me out of the hole and feed me, but as soon as he left they stuck me right

45

back in. When I came out after ten days, I was skin and bones and back in stripes and chains. I overheard the conversation between the screw that shot me and the camp Captain.

"If you let that S.O.B. Watson have one visit or get one letter or do *anything*, I'm gonna quit. That guy's a wild animal!"

"Watson's been in the hole," the Captain growled at him. "He's in stripes and chains, he's lost any good time he'd piled up, and he's been shot. How much more punishment d'ya think he needs, wild animal or not? I remind you, Mister, I'm runnin' this camp. When you want to leave, you know the way out." First time I ever heard of a Captain having any kind of a heart.

When Angie, good old Angie, came to see me Sunday, they let her in, and I saw the guard heading down the road with his bag. I waved good-by and he thumbed his nose, so I did the same. Angie didn't say one word about I-told-you-so.

We had some way-out cats at that camp. One we called Stud because he had a twelve- or thirteen-inch dick. He got sent up for screwing his own grandmother. He had pointed out the window so she would go to see what he was looking at. He pulled the window down on the old lady, flipped up her dress in the back, and put everything he had into her ass, and that was plenty. I know that gilflestered her, as the saying goes. This cat would play with his pecker all the time. I guess that's what made it so big.

I bet on Jersey Joe against Ezzard Charles and won. The guy who lost didn't like it, so I had to hit him in the mouth. Took sixteen stitches. And a friend of his didn't like that, so they both pulled knives on me. I pulled mine, and it was a standoff. Captain came in and told us to put away the knives. If we wanted to fight, use our fists.

"O.K.!" I said. "I'll take on both of you at once!"

"No go. You're too good with your fists."

"I got chains on my feet. That ought to make it up."

But one of them was the Captain's boy, so they put me in the hole anyway. After about five days he asked me if I could whip a guy from over at Whittier Prison Camp who was good with the gloves. I told him I could try, and the guards and prisoners from both camps started laying bets. I went back to work in the rock hole, but before I could fight the guy some rocks fell on me and broke my left hand. Captain wouldn't let me fight one-handed. A year or so later I met up with the guy and beat the hell out of him.

One of the boys managed to get hold of some hacksaw blades, and we started sawing through a window, but some-one ratted on us. Back to the hole. By that time I was bitter against anyone who carried a badge and a gun. Even thinking about it and hearing those damn, heavy boots would set me into a rage. I was mad enough to tear up the Gideon Bible and a little magazine called *The Upper Room* that they sometimes stuck in the hole with us to give us consolation. *Consolation,* my ass. It was a long time before I ever opened one of them. To *read,* that is.

When I got out that time, I found the rat and beat holy hell out of him. They didn't think the hole was bad enough then, so they hung me up with handcuffs in a ring on the wall of the sick room. I stayed hung up for seventy-four hours without eating or sleeping. A few hours more than three days. My wrists swelled up around the cuffs, and my feet puffed up so bad they broke the shoestrings.

I had only two thoughts. *Get away. Get even.*

One of the guys at the camp told me if I could get fifty bucks he would get me a gun. "I'll get the fifty," I said.

So when Angie came to see me, this cat and his visitor sat right next to me and passed me a .38 short-barrel Smith and

Wesson. When you get back to the cell, they always shake you down. I put the .38 inside my shirt—I was still in stripes and chains. Angie had brought me some cake and candy, so when it came my turn to be searched, I dropped everything on the floor. The guards helped me pick it up and forgot to frisk me.

Next day I had the gun with me and got it past the screw at the gate. What I didn't know was that one of the guys was scared I'd kill that Minus-Zero foreman we all hated, so he told the Captain about the gun.

When we got to the rock hole, three guards held their guns on me. "Out there on that rock, Watson! You heard me! Sit down on that rock out in the middle, away from everyone."

Another guard yelled at the rest of them. "Stay away, all of you! Back!" I went and sat down in the center of the rock hole. Four or five more guards came, took the .38, and told me to get into the dog wagon. I looked the foreman straight in the eye.

"Bastard! This is your lucky day! I hope you know it!" He did. So did everyone else.

One guy stuck with me; he said he didn't want to stay in such a sorry place with such sorry people. They loaded us up in the dog wagon, took us off to Craggy Prison Camp at Asheville for ten more glorious days of sun-and-fun in the hole there, then to Burnsville and another rock hole. This was in 1948. I was twenty-six.

Was I getting away? Was I getting even? In those days Burnsville was called the outlaw camp, a tough place for tough men. A ratfink couldn't survive in those cell blocks. The honor-grade prisoners ate in another mess because if one was caught in the mess hall with the gun prisoners—the A-, B-, and C-grade prisoners always under armed guard—he got a real beating. The Captain would call one of the gun-grade prisoners out to the office at night, then four or five honor-graders would be waiting to beat him up while the guards looked the other way. Soon as we got hold of one of the honor-graders we'd pay him back, with interest. The guards were afraid to try to break it up.

The guards at Burnsville were tough. Had to be, I guess. In the forties they were mostly farmers without any education, hired only because they were expert shots. They'd deal out harsh punishment for any infraction of the rules, most of which they made up themselves. When the State issued shoes for the prisoners, the guards would wear them out first. We always had sore feet from wearing old, broken-down shoes that didn't fit.

They did feed us good because they worked us ten hours a day on the rock pile, winter and summer.

There were three segregation holes side by side, right outside the regular cell block. A corridor ran the length of the building, and the screws would go along that corridor peeking through the slits in the steel doors to see if we were still alive, not that they cared. They'd sometimes sneak up to the wall to hear what we were saying, so we'd really lay it on about them, their families, and their ancestry. They'd pay us back by not giving us water for two or three days at a stretch.

Prisoners who were not in the hole figured out a way to get food to prisoners who were. We'd make a long arrow out of a welding rod, tie a strong cord to it, and shoot it across the corridor toward the hole. There was just enough room under the steel doors to put your hand and arm about halfway out, depending on your size. We'd keep shooting the arrow until the guy in the hole could reach it. He could then pull it into his cell.

We'd flatten down packages of cigarettes and food and tie them to the end of the cord so they could be pulled under the door. Sometimes that was the only way a guy could survive.

When a man was about to come out of the hole, we'd take up a collection among the prisoners who had any money. We'd divide it among the ones in the hole so they could buy themselves some milk and eggs and other food that was easy on their stomachs until they could get used to eating regular food again. It might take two or three days before a man's stomach was in shape.

Back in the forties they wouldn't mail your letters home or to the courts, especially if you were a troublemaker. They didn't want anyone on the outside to know the treatment we got on the chain gang or any of the other conditions.

There were always old magazines and papers around, so we would write our letters and roll them up in those old papers. As our squad truck passed a group of school children, we would toss the magazines or papers out to them, and they would mail the letters for us. The squad truck is one that has a trailer on the back with an armed guard. If you tried to jump out, you could jump right into the guard's gun barrel, but he couldn't stop us from throwing out old papers.

We had been hearing about a woman judge appointed by Governor Kerr Scott, named Miss Susie Sharp. Some prisoner was bringing charges against a Captain of a camp somewhere upstate, claiming the Captain had had the man hung up in a steel ring on the wall for sixty-two hours. I had hung seventy-four hours! It may be hard to believe, but even being in the hole without food and sometimes water is more humane than hanging up on a ring on the wall, no matter how long.

Hanging there with your feet just off the floor, your face mashed against the wall, your wrists and ankles breaking, does something horrible to your mind as well as to your body. This judge, who was shocked about the stuff she was hearing, gave us some hope. Some of us would write to her and describe the bad conditions and the brutal treatment we were getting.

Sometimes our letters would be rolled up in comic books—one sure way to get the kids to unroll them. It took a while, but some of our letters must have reached her. The day came when at least they fed us in the hole. That was in 1949.

One of the roads that went through the rock hole where we were working was a popular place for motorists to slow down and watch us. Sometimes the rubberneckers got more than they bargained for. When the men needed to go to the toilet, the guards were afraid to let them go behind rocks or other hiding places for fear they would escape. So they forced us to go to the edge of the road to relieve ourselves. We didn't mind it so much when the people going past were just the usual squares, whom we despised, but when it was a bunch of young kids, we hated it. As hardened as all of us were to prison and prison ways, it embarrassed the shit out of us to be caught with our pants down, so we'd pull our shirts up over our heads so they couldn't tell who we were.

Well, back in the forties and the early fifties, that was the State's way of "rehabilitating" men who got into trouble. One change I do remember, though. They stopped calling us *convicts* and tried calling us *prisoners*. It was a long time before the word *inmate* was used.

It took even longer to get anyone to see that under severe punishment we would not lie down and let ourselves be run over without trying to retaliate. Our biggest problem was that we were outnumbered.

There are some good men in prison, believe it or not. Decent-minded and brave as any soldier in war, braver than some. I've seen men do things behind bars that they would receive a medal for if they were in military service during a war. I don't trust these people who never make mistakes and who look down their noses at anyone who does. I respect courage wherever it is. And not just gun-courage.

51

Funny, Angie always showed up. She'd ride through that road across the rock hole on a motorcycle and wave at me. They figured she might get a gun to me, so they loaded me on the dog wagon again and took me to Central Prison in Raleigh. I was on lockup for a month, and every day they tried to find out where I got that .38. They thought it was from Angie, but it wasn't.

When they sent me east to the camp at Greenville, North Carolina, she wrote me every day and came to see me every visiting Sunday just like at Franklin, although it was a couple of hundred miles. I was there eighteen months; then they sent me to Raleigh for a suit of clothes and on to Craggy Prison in Asheville for release. A great day!

Angie was waiting. We were married the afternoon of the day I got out, October 25, 1950. We had waited a damn long time.

Pretty soon one of my stepsons started giving me trouble. He would mistreat his mother, so I told him to stop it. He knew I could beat him, so he waited until my back was turned and stabbed me between the ribs with a switchblade knife. I caught his hand with the knife, and he jerked away from me. I grabbed a shotgun and started after him, but I was bleeding so bad I couldn't keep going. I had a big hole in my back and a cut in my chest, but I wouldn't go to the hospital because of the police.

"I'll take care of that boy myself!" I told Angie. "Can't have those damn cops here!"

"Now, Frank, lie down and let me fix you up." She started cleaning off the blood and putting bandages on me. She was so scared for her boy that she was shaking like all get-out. I was hurt so bad I couldn't get out of bed for four days. When I did, I grabbed the shotgun again and started out the door.

"Frank, honey! *Frank!* Don't hurt him! He's just a kid!" She hung on to me, crying and yelling.

"Kid, hell! He's a damn killer! He almost got me!"

Finally, I cooled off. After all he was her boy, and we were just married and all. But then the F.B.I. came poking around for him for jumping parole.

A neighbor had told them about him stabbing me. I knew where he was. The F.B.I. kept after me, and poor Angie nearly had a breakdown. Finally, I'd had enough.

"I wouldn't give you guys the time of day. Beat it!" I told them. "I'll skin my own cats. I don't call the cops about *any-thing*, y'hear? Don't come around here any more." So they left.

But the neighbor fingered the boy for them, and they sent him to the Federal Prison at Lewisburg, Pennsylvania. I took Angie up there to see him, and then we went around by Norfolk, Virginia, where I got a job on a fireboat. I stuck with it for six months, going straight and working hard because of Angie.

The crew asked me to beat up the captain of the boat, Ol' Cap'n Bligh, they called him. Everybody hated him. He was a mighty hard man to work for. I agreed because I hated him too. We had some words and he took a swing at me, so I beat him up bad.

The F.B.I. got in on that too because it happened on government property, but they let me go because he hit me first. I had plenty of witnesses.

Angie was glad that I got out of their clutches. I'd already done too much time for her tastes.

7

ANGIE DESERVES A HELL OF A LOT OF CREDIT FOR TRYING TO GET me straightened around. First she stuck by me through all those months in prison before we got married; then she decided we'd better settle down in Asheville, get a decent house to live in, go to church, see a movie, act like ordinary squares.

I'd sit beside her at the Baptist Church, but I'd hardly hear what the preacher was saying. My grandfather Cook was as real as if he'd come into the room, pounding away on his homemade pulpit, hollering about sin and salvation. When Grandfather Cook used to ask if we were washed of our sins, I'd look at my hands and decide I was as washed of sin as I'd ever be, and then I'd go back to sleep on Granny's lap.

Angie said that church did her a lot of good. She'd had a pretty hard life, and if it helped her I was willing to see if it would help me too. Her husbands had been rotten to her. I wasn't much better. Her kids didn't turn out too good. It was sad. I wanted to do everything I could to make up to her for caring about me and sticking with me. Going to church with her was a way of thanking her.

I can't remember anyone else in all those years who really cared one whit about me. Really cared. Certainly not Betty Sue. She'd been glad to get rid of me. People are damn lucky to have anyone who gives a damn about them—it means they matter to someone. Nothing else is more important.

I wanted Angie to have everything in this world that she deserved, so that's probably why we soon ran short of money.

I'd slip out and hold up a hamburger joint or some drunk—not much of anything—but it tore her up.

"Don't do it, Frank! We'll get along. Why are you doing this, Frank? Ain't you had enough trouble?"

"Listen, Angie, they don't catch Frank Watson! I'm too smart for them. And I never do hurt anyone unless I have to. You just stop worrying about me. I'm a great big boy and I can take care of myself. And you too. That's my job now, to take care of you."

Being able to say that made me feel real good. Me taking care of Angie.

When things got real tight, I'd go to Norfolk or Newport News and get a safe or knock off a finance company. I took about eight trips up there and four or five to Georgia. I lost track of all the safes I got in Asheville. I could have opened a store.

One day five cops came to the house to get Angie's son for jumping parole. The same neighbor had tipped them off. It wasn't the first time they had come, nor the first time she had fingered him. Angie would tell me how the police had walked in, pushed her aside, and searched the house without a warrant.

This time I was home. They came to both doors, front and back. My stepson was begging me to protect him. I got my German Luger, jacked a shell into the chamber, and told Angie to open the door. I was standing right behind her.

"Whattaya want?" She was shaking with fright.

"We're here to search your house. We're hunting for your son."

I stepped out and faced them. "You got a warrant?"

"We don't need a warrant. We're coming in anyway. We want that kid."

One of them reached to open the screen door.

"The hell you are!" I pulled my gun. "The first guy that sets foot in my house is going to get his head blown off!" One of them reached for his gun. "I warn you. I'll kill you!"

Still another was trying to come in the back door, so I swung my gun on him too. "Get the hell out of my house and off my property! Every damn one of you! I'll drop some of you!" They knew I meant business because they began scrambling for their car. As soon as they left, I got the boy into my car and took him to a friend's house out in the country.

Asheville got kind of hot, so we bought a house trailer and had it moved to Charlotte. I was doing pretty good holding up stores in Gastonia, especially getting guns and ammunition. My stepson and I would go out in the woods for target practice. We both got good at shooting from the hip with shotguns, rifles, and pistols. It was fun.

One afternoon I was stretched out in the back room of the trailer reading a book—probably *From Here to Eternity*, a great book, believe me—when I heard a racket out front. The F.B.I., the State Patrol, and some city cops had surrounded the trailer and come in and were putting the cuffs on Angie's boy. They didn't want me—or said they didn't—until they began looking through the trailer and finding all those weapons. They took me in, and Angie too. Then they laid it on me.

"We've got the warrant for your wife, Watson," one of them said, "but if you're willing to tell us the straight truth about where you got all this loot, we'll tear it up. Otherwise, you're both going in the clink because we'll get her for receiving stolen goods."

"O.K., O.K. Tear it up." When I told him about the stash of guns I had in Asheville and took him to them, I got my sentence cut from ten-to-fifteen down to four-to-seven years.

My stepson was already on Federal probation, so he got sent to Atlanta. I ended up back at Central Prison in Raleigh. It was November, 1953. In a month I'd be thirty-two years old.

A bad go-round with malaria hit me almost at once. I'd had it ever since Arkansas. I passed out twice before they got me to the hospital; then the doctor came around and asked me what kind of drugs I was using.

I was too sick to talk, just shook my head and groaned. He blew his stack and ordered them to pump out my stomach. You ever had your stomach pumped? Don't.

A couple of the boys later told off the doc. "Listen, Doc, Frank Watson won't put any kind of drug or medicine down his gullet unless some medic shoves it there. He's afraid of that stuff."

"Frank Watson afraid of medicine? Something *scares* him?" He started to laugh. "Maybe I'd better go see him." So he came around. "Sorry about pumping out your belly, Watson," he said. "The way you were acting, I was sure it was drugs."

"Well, Doc, if you'd listened—"

"Listened? You weren't talking. Just wagging your head."

"I was too sick to talk. You should have been able to see that."

"Right. And I'm real sorry. If it had taken those guys another ten minutes to haul you into the hospital, you'd have been dead. Ten minutes at the outside. Feeling better?"

"Yeah, some. It would help if I could walk around a little. I ain't used to loafing like this."

He sat there and looked at me for a minute. "Watson, they say you won't put anything on your insides that isn't recommended by a doctor. You must be a rare bird. I don't know anyone like that. From what I've heard, you're not scared of anything else. How come?"

"I'm not scared of anything on the outside, Doc, anything I can see working. That I can handle. But I don't like sneaky things—I can't see what happens on the inside. I'm just a damn practical man."

When I got out to Halifax Prison Camp from Central, they'd

just had a big riot. Everything was in an uproar. They put me on the roads, and the Captain kept riding me to make me work harder. I told him I was weak as a cat, just out of the hospital with malaria, and he laughed and said, "Get on it, or it's the hole fer ya!"

"Cap, if you bother me one more time, I'll take my pick-handle and knock off your damn head!" So that night I landed in the hole.

The State Patrol came back and surrounded the place. Someone had tried to kill the dog-boy, an honor-grader who handled the dogs and tried to catch prisoners who escaped. We hated the Captain, of course, but we despised the dog-boys. It's a wonder they weren't all murdered, just because of their jobs. But then they carried guns. That made a difference.

If you plan to escape, you have to be scientific. First find out the lay of the land. I worked on a bridge gang repairing bridges; that way I got to know the whole county in about three months. Next gather up escape money. This has to be done through a "solid" prisoner, one you can trust. He takes up a collection from all the solid ones in camp. It's a business agreement. If you succeed, you don't owe anyone anything. If you fail, you have to pay it all back. The collector keeps a record.

Then you've got to find out the State Patrol schedule, the time they're on duty, the time they're off, what their routes are and all that. In the early fifties, they all knocked off at midnight.

When my buddy Johnny and I were ready to escape from Halifax, I noticed that the trucks always slowed down on a certain hill. That's where we jumped off. He landed O.K., but I hit one knee on the blacktop and busted it wide open. I had to drag that leg along behind me, hurting like hell.

It was hot as hell too, August, 1954. All the creeks and water holes were dried up. They got the dogs from three counties to trail us. The guy with me lost his nerve—said we'd have to have water and food someway or we'd die.

"Listen, man," I told him, "you're not giving up until we both get away. Then I don't give a hootin' damn what you do."

"Frank, those fucking dogs are so close I could hit 'em with a rock!"

"*Hit 'em!* But shut up! They can't smell us because it's so hot. Don't give us away by your damn yacking."

Four days we stayed in the woods and lived on wild grapes and apples. It's always better to run in the summer when there's some food to be had.

We tried to get a car once, but the guy saw us, so we had to duck. Then we tried again. The people were in the front room playing bridge, and there was a 1950 Buick four-door out front. Johnny lost his nerve and hid down the street. I was pretty fed up with him by that time.

"Well, are you gonna help me or ain't ya?"

"I never stole a car, Frank!"

"Ya done enough other stuff! Now put up or shut up!"

If the people had even turned their heads they would have seen us, but we shoved the car down a little hill and straight-wired it. The boy got in, and we headed toward Asheville.

The damn crate belonged to a cop! I found his nightstick and ticket book and threw them into a creek. The thing had just been overhauled, but I drove it so fast I burned the motor up.

You'd probably never guess where I hid out in Asheville. Thomas Wolfe's old cabin! And in a kind of tree house above the recreation park. I always liked to read Thomas Wolfe. It felt real romantic to be up there where no one would have thought of looking for me. I should have stayed. Might have learned something. He might have written some of his famous novels there!

The cabin was a great hideaway. It had four rooms and not

59

much furniture. It was at the end of a winding road and it was hidden by huge oak trees. Thick woods all around. There was a homemade ladder nailed to a tree so you could climb up to the tree house.

I found a pair of candlesticks there, kind of interesting, glass, made in the shape of seals. Instead of holding up balls with their noses the way real seals did, they held up candles. I gave them to Angie.

She'd cook and bring up food every day; then she heard I'd been cornered in a shoot-out. That must have been the Malvern Hill drug store holdup I pulled. I took the safe up there and opened it. It was full of pills and morphine that I later sold in Charlotte for a nice haul. People around Asheville still remember that holdup more than any of the others I pulled. It got so I was afraid to sleep in the cabin, so I'd take some blankets that Angie brought me and sleep in the woods. One thing I did find in that safe was a diamond brooch—I thought it was glass, so I gave it away. Of course, there was money, too, and some books of old coins that I didn't have any way of selling.

Johnny had already beat it to Charlotte so he could marry his girl; then he later testified against me in court. Well, win a few—

Once again I didn't have a car or money. Time to get on the stick. There was a Mr. X in Charlotte whose nephew was in prison with me. His business was bad, so we made a deal. When customers with money came into his store he'd finger them for me. One of them, he said, always carried four or five thousand dollars on him and wore a big diamond worth at least a thousand.

He wasn't home, so I broke in the back door and waited for him in the kitchen, dressed in a mask, a hat, and a topcoat. Mr. X hadn't told me the guy was shacking up with a telephone operator—maybe he didn't know it—but that night he brought her home with him.

When the man went into the bedroom, she came to the kitchen. I threw down on her with my pistol. "Into the bedroom! Quick! No back talk!"

All she did was scream like crazy.

"Shut up, or I'll blast your head off!" I followed her into the bedroom. The man saw me, and it liked to have scared the pants off him.

"Don't shoot! Don't shoot!" He was shaking all over, just like in a movie. "Here, take my wallet. You can have what's in it. Don't shoot!"

Damn coward, I thought to myself. She'd be better off without him, money or no money. I got about four hundred bucks and a .38 he had in his pocket. Mr. X hadn't told me about that. Must have carried it to protect his wad. I forgot the damn ring. It would have been right nice to give to Angie. Look pretty on her.

"All right, you two. Into the living room. On the floor! Flat down! No, don't try the phone. I pulled the wires."

"Don't shoot! Don't shoot!" the bastard was still whining.

"Shut your mouth or I will! I hate that damn squawking!"

The next guy was in Mr. X's store. I followed the square to the john, threw my gun on him, made him kneel down with his head in the toilet. He had about a thousand bucks on him. I walked to my car in the parking lot and drove away. It was working great.

Next I threw my gun on a guy in his car and forced him to drive me outside of town, where I robbed him and made him lie down in a ditch.

When I went back to split up with Mr. X, he'd lost his nerve. Said the place was filling up with cops and he couldn't stand that or his business would fold.

61

"'I know I can trust you to bring me my share, Watson, but it's just one of those things that I think I'd better lay off for a while. No hard feelings, I hope?"

"None at all, Mr. X. Nice knowin' ya."

Even then, he fingered a poker game with several thousand in the pot, but I didn't get there. Some of those cops sniffing around his place were bound to stumble on me when my back was turned.

8

I just missed a haul of $87,000, but it was o.k. because they got the guys and sent them up for twenty years. I'd been shot by a night watchman in Charlotte. The bullet went clear through my leg, so I got on a bus for Asheville, where I knew there was a doctor who would fix me up and keep his lip buttoned. If I hadn't got caught in Asheville, I'd have been back in Charlotte to help out on that $87,000 job.

I dropped off the bus in Biltmore and dragged myself to a corner service station to phone Angie. While I was waiting for a cab, an off-duty policeman spotted me. When I saw the cruiser coming, I went to the men's room, but they followed me and called for me to come out. I didn't answer, so they sent in a guy I knew to knock on the door and tell me they had the place surrounded.

"The cops are afraid to open the door, Frank," he said, laughing. "They think you have a gun, and they know you can use it."

"I do have one, but it's in my bag. I don't have it on me."

Of course they found it. Then they asked about my leg.

"Fell and hurt it. It's nothing. Just a scratch."

At the police station the blood was oozing out through the towel I'd got in the men's room, even through my pants, and dripping on the floor into little puddles. I was probably turning kind of green too. They took me to the hospital, got me sewed up, and put me in a room with a guard on the door.

"You're lucky to be alive, man," the doctor said.

"I hear that kind of talk all the time, Doc."

"That bullet just missed a big artery. Another half hour and you'd have been gone, bled to death."

"Last close squeak was ten minutes, Doc. Be a big loss if the time got down to nothing, wouldn't it?"

"Yes, of course. I hope you're going to get along all right."

I just laughed. I tried hard to think who'd be really teed off if I winked out. Angie, probably. The State maybe, because I owed them so much time on their rock piles. How would they get all those big boulders broken up without Frank Watson's big brawny shoulders and strong back? After all, you have to keep the government going somehow. And the squares have to be able to drive along the highways in their big shiny cars.

They kept me in the hospital about four hours; then they got a dog wagon with a mattress and carried me off to Craggy Prison overnight and on back to Central in Raleigh. Old Home Week.

The hospital sent the State a bill for eighty dollars for fixing me up. The guys at Central Prison hit the roof. It was great.

When I got well enough, they sent me back to Halifax, tried me for escape, and sent me to Nash Prison Camp, near Nashville, N. C., to serve out my time, plus a year added for escape, but they did agree to let it run concurrently.

That's where I first met Red Eye Meadows. He probably had a real first name, but I never knew it. He's dead now. Red Eye was the toughest Captain in the prison system, but I will say that he always kept his word. That's more than I can say for a lot of prison officials. They'll tell you any kind of lie rather than give you a straight yes or no. You can't respect a guy like that.

Red Eye was a hard man. He'd killed four or five prisoners and shot up I don't know how many more. And Nash was a hard camp; that's why they had him there. He put me in the bull gang, about twenty of us, all hard rock, always in trouble with the guards. Red Eye wouldn't have a guard in his camp who hadn't killed at least one prisoner.

When we'd get off the truck, the guard would call out a couple of our names and say something like, "Listen, you bastards, Cap'n Meadows says that if you try to run or give us one bit of trouble, we're not to bring ya in walkin'. Dead is the word. Feet first. Got it?"

State policy says that guards are not allowed to swear at prisoners, but they came mighty close to it and used a lot of imagination. The really foul-mouthed ones were the detectives and the police. I'd hear new and fouler stuff every time one of them picked me up.

After one of those big welcome speeches, I'd give the screw one of my go-to-hell grins. He'd know I was working on a way to escape. I always was.

Nash work gangs had two guards plus a foreman and a truck driver, all armed. When we stopped, the driver would head for the woods so he could catch us there if we slipped past the guards. Boxed in, that's what they thought we were.

The worst of it was that we were in swamps with water up to our chests, every kind of snake, including moccasins and copperheads, flies, mosquitoes, stinging insects, mud, sink-holes, stench. We'd cut trees in the swamp and carry them to a truck on the road. When we'd get through the day without being snake-bit, we'd get back to the camp, muddy and tired and stinkin', but we couldn't get any clean clothes. I always like to keep myself clean when I can, so I'd shower and wash out my muddy duds and hope the stuff would dry overnight.

It was hot as hell in the swamps. You couldn't breathe. And then to have Red Eye Meadows' foreman on you for more work, more work, how could you help hating everyone? We were all bitter and mad, full of hate. It was like poison, and it never changed.

Once in a while a man with heart trouble would come in, with a paper from his doctor saying so, but Red Eye would tear up the paper and laugh in his face. "I'm runnin' this camp, bastard!" That was Red Eye's slogan.

So during the day, the guy would fall out from the heat and the heavy work, and we'd carry him out on a board. If he lived, Red Eye would have him transferred to another camp.

A boy came to me and wanted me to help him grab a guard on the cell block at night. Some of us were in C-grade stripes and leg-irons, but he knew I had the chains fixed so we could get them off fast. His plan sounded O.K. until I found out who was in on it with him—three of the worst finks in the state.

"Those three guys are rotten, kid," I told him. "Any time you try to get away, you got to be able to trust your buddies. They'll fink on you, those cats. I'm givin' it to you straight."

"No, Frank, they're O.K. I'm sure of it. They're good guys, all of 'em."

So he tried it. The guard opened the door to turn a man in, and the kid grabbed him. Sure enough, the rats left him cold. The second guard was outside checking windows and came running in and tried to shoot the boy. The first guard didn't have a gun, but this one did. We could get cold drinks in bottles there, so two of us threw bottles at his head and chased him outside, bleeding and yelling. The kid ran from the other guard and hid in the cell block.

So here came Red Eye and his goon squad, seven or eight of them, with shotguns and rifles, shooting up the cell block. The men in the cells got under the bunks. I squatted down beside a foot locker, and the kid came and pushed up against me, scared and crying.

"They're gonna kill me, Frank! They're fixin' to kill me! Help me! Help me!"

"They won't kill ya," I said. But I wasn't sure.

"Hey, you," they started hollering. "Come out with your hands up and we won't hurt ya!"

So he went out. He was so young. About like me when I was at the orphanage, just a green, lost kid. They lit into him with their pistol butts. When he was unconscious, they dragged him around where we couldn't see him, and then they shot four times in the air to make us think they had killed him.

We found out that he lived. They stuck him in the hole with no food until he healed up enough to go back to work. Never trust rats.

The word got out that Red Eye Meadows would take over Ivy Bluff Prison Camp when they got it done. *Escape-Proof* they were calling it, *Little Alcatraz*. About that time they called about ten of us in to Raleigh and asked what camp we wanted to go to. Captain King, who would take over at Nash from Meadows, didn't want us.

"Don't make no difference to me," I told them. "I've been in all your screwed-up camps, and I can tell you this, one ain't no worse'n any other."

"Possibly Lincolnton? O.K.?"

"Sure, why not? I'll get out sooner or later, one way or another, night or day, winter or summer, rain or shine." And I grinned at him real friendly.

"Not while we have an eye on you, bud."

"Watch the papers."

It was the night before Thanksgiving, 1955. I was stretched out on my bunk reading, some book called *The Grapes of Wrath*. I worked through that one four or five times. I understood those Okies. Four guys came over and asked me if I wanted to leave right then.

"Sure! I'm always ready to leave."

The guard had his back to us. He was talking to a man in the other cell block. The second guard was in the mess hall drinking coffee. By that time I'd gotten a homemade key from a guy who was afraid to use it. I eased it into the lock, opened the door, and we all raced across and grabbed the guard. While the other four held him, I checked the outside. All clear. But the guard had gotten his hands on the bars, and those four guys couldn't pry him loose. I walked over, hooked him in the short ribs, yanked him off the bars, and dumped him inside the cell block doors.

"Anyone else want to go with us?" I yelled in. "Step on it!"

Some had life, some had twenty-five and thirty years, and they were all scared; so I locked the door, and we went outside and over the fence into the woods. Two of the boys went off together and were picked up at home. Clyde and Leroy went with me. It was a dark night, so we could move without being seen. The screws were yelling themselves blue in the face and making a big ruckus, turning on the bright lights—a regular hullabaloo.

We stayed in the woods three days. My feet were in terrible shape. We never had shoes that fit, so I had big blisters on my feet. I couldn't wear shoes for a month after that breakout. I had to slide around in some old house slippers.

We went to a store and stole some food and clothing, two shotguns, a rifle, and shells; then we got a car from a nearby farmhouse and set out for Leroy's granddaddy's farm in Georgia. Going through Greenville, South Carolina, the police fell in behind us. I was in the back seat about half asleep.

"*Hey!* Leroy! Why you stoppin'?"

"Cops!"

"Wait till they get out of the car; then drive like hell!" I put shells in the shotgun, but I didn't have to use it. The night was foggy and we lost them at the edge of town on a fast curve, but we near-bout turned over going so fast. Leroy was a good driver.

We stayed in Georgia for a while and got rested up; then we went back to North Carolina, pulled off a couple of jobs to get some cash, and went to Clyde's daddy's place. We parked on a side road so he could walk to his house to get some clothes and a gun. He came back pretty scared.

"The place is crawling with screws from Lincolnton Prison Camp," he said. "Let's get out of here!"

We tried to back the car out of that little road, but we got stuck on the ice. Finally we told Clyde to stay there, and Leroy and I went down the road to a farmhouse and got the farmer and his son out of bed.

"Sorry to trouble you, sirs," I said with my best manners, "but me and my friend here are guards from Lincolnton Prison Camp, and we're stuck down here in the woods. Could you maybe help us out? It's very important."

"Sure 'nuf," the farmer said, pulling on his pants and a warm jacket. "I heered they was huntin' a couple escapers up this way. Is one of 'em Clyde?" I didn't answer.

"Sure do hate t'bother y'all," I said when we got outside where it was dark. "But I figgered you'd rather help us than let those prisoners get away."

"Right! Where you stuck?"

I motioned down the road, and he got his tractor, hooked on to us, and pulled us out of there and onto the gravel, where we could get some traction. Clyde was hiding in the bushes.

"Thanks a million!" I called out the window to the farmer. "If you'll just come up to the prison camp office in the mornin', they'll be glad to pay you. Sure did hate to get you nice people out of bed!"

Clyde, Leroy, and I struck out for Morganton and took a

room at a boarding house. I told the landlady we'd been hunting and that's why my feet were in such bad shape. Could she fix me a hot salt-water bath for them? She did, and it felt so good, sitting there soaking my dogs.

Leroy and Clyde went off trying to find a place in town where we could pull a job. When they came back, we were sitting there talking when I heard a car outside. I peeked through the blinds. It was a police car. The woman's daughter had been suspicious of us and reported us. And our guns were locked in the trunk of our car.

Bare, wet feet and all, I grabbed my things and told the boys to come with me. We went out the front door while the cops were out back taking down the license number on our car. We hid behind some trees down the street. I'd already frostbitten my feet a couple of years before; this icy cold scared me for a while, but it wasn't long until the cops pulled out. We scrammed for our car and got out of there, headed for Georgia.

We drove around through three or four states hunting a safe place. Up near Canton, North Carolina, a paper mill town, the police fell in behind us. We were doing over a hundred. I lowered the window and fired two shotgun shells into the police car. That stopped them.

I took the wheel because I knew the country. The back way into Asheville was through Enka Bridge, but even there they were already setting up a road block. I went past them at a hundred miles an hour and cut through Pisgah Forest to the Hendersonville highway. Then I drove along the river road to Short Michigan Avenue in Asheville, where Angie lived, and hid the car behind my own house.

Angie gave me some big hugs and kisses, but that didn't last very long. "Pitt Sluder said he was going to shoot you on sight, Frank."

"The Chief of Police?"

"Yes."

"He's a big talker, Pitt is."

"He really said it, Frank. And he means it. You aren't safe here."

"This is a free country, ain't it? A man ought to be safe in his own home. You just tell your friend Pitt Sluder that he can come out a-shootin'!" I put my arms around her again, but she wouldn't have any of it.

"You ain't safe, Frank. Not here. Not anywhere."

9

WHAT ANGIE TOLD ME MADE ME PLENTY MAD. PITT SLUDER MUST think he could scare me. Why? And Angie was downright cold, for the first time ever.

I slammed out of the house, and the three of us—Leroy and Clyde and I—headed over to Clingman's Avenue to the Colonial Bakery. They had a lot of money there on Thursdays and Fridays, I'd heard from a man who worked there. We climbed over the fence at the back and saw a man loading trucks with pies, cakes, and bread. I walked up behind him quietly, let him turn around and see me.

"Don't say nothin'. Git into this little room and lie down." I shoved him inside the building. "You guys, tie him up."

Through a screen door I saw three or four men eating lunch. I stepped into the room, threw down on them with my sawed-off shotgun, and told them to line up against the wall.

"Don't let him fool you!" one of them said to the others. "He's just got a toy gun and is trying to scare hell out of us."

I clicked the safety. It made a right loud noise. "Now, shut up and do as I say!"

"Do what he says, idiots! That's a real gun! He ain't foolin'!"

They'd just been paid, so we got a nice haul out of their pockets. I had Leroy hold a gun on them while I checked the office. The door was locked, so I kicked it in. The safe was small and would have been easy to open if I'd had a little time.

"Clyde, go see about the one we tied up."

He came back on the double. "He ain't there! He's got himself untied, and he's gone!"

"That means the police— You guys against the wall, git down on the floor! Don't move for five full minutes or we'll be back to see you."

The safe was too much to carry, so we climbed the fence and got out of town fast. The whole job got us about five hundred dollars. I sure hated to leave that safe. We'd have been on Easy Street with that payroll.

On the way to Georgia again, I bought a snub-nosed .38 Smith and Wesson in Greenville, S.C. When we got to Leroy's granddaddy's place, they were all scared of us. The dumb kid showed his new gun to everyone and bragged that we had escaped from a chain gang. The little boys around there ate it up and passed the story on, so of course the police showed up.

The police were like cockroaches. When we'd stop for gas, someone would call them. We'd try to eat, and there'd be a cop. At one grub-stop, the owner and two other guys, all of them with guns, waited out front for us. His wife and daughter were serving us our lunch inside.

"Stay where you are until I honk the horn," I told Leroy and Clyde. "That's the signal I'm ready." I knew those guys outside wouldn't do anything as long as my two boys were in the restaurant with the women.

I went out real easy, got in the car, started it, and stuck the shotgun out the window as I honked the horn. The boys scrambled out, jumped into the car, and we took off.

Those other three characters didn't dare move. We had two shotguns and a rifle in the car. I figured they'd seen them when they were out snooping around. We hid for a while, then we went into Marietta, Georgia, to buy three caps to disguise ourselves for a holdup of a meat packing company.

"Leroy, you go do the shopping while Clyde and I wait in

the car on this side street. Come to think of it, I got married in this town once. I was really young and green then."

Sure enough, cops. They went up to a filling station and turned around so they could come back and get a better look at us. I was going to do a U-turn in the street and head out of town, but the damn car stalled right in the middle of the turn. There we sat, crossways of the street, lots of traffic because it was Saturday, horns blaring at us. I ground away on the starter with my gun in one hand while Clyde got more scared.

Just before the police car got to us, the motor caught. I revved it up and streaked for open country, the cops right behind me, siren whining.

"What about Leroy, Frank? You ain't gonna leave him?"

"Later. We'll think about Leroy later. Keep your head down."

When we came to a steep hill, I waited until a big truck was coming right at us from the other way; then I pulled out of line and put five cars between me and the police. The truck had to slow down to keep from hitting us. I could hear the brakes squealing, and I'll bet that driver was doing some damn fancy cussing. I was laughing. We shook the police and went out into the country to wait for dark; then we went back to town to hunt for Leroy. No luck.

"Can't stick around here any longer, kid," I said. "Let's find a drive-in movie up country someplace and get some shuteye."

When we got to one that had four shows and stayed open all night, I dropped off to sleep, but Clyde watched the whole shebang.

"You must be gittin' old, Frank. Can't stay awake for a movie!"

"Knock it off!"

By the time we got to Murphy, North Carolina, the next day, he was begging me to let him off. I found out later that

74

he and Leroy had been wanting to shake me ever since I shot at the police car in Canton. "We'd better leave Frank. He's gonna get us killed!" they'd been telling each other, but they were too scared of me to ask me to let them go. I opened the door and told him goodby. He seemed mighty relieved.

Between Canton and Asheville I saw a girl walking along the highway. It was raining hard. It must have been about midnight.

"Need a ride, young lady?"

"Could be."

"It's mighty wet tonight. And late for a little girl like you to be out!"

"Yeah."

"Hop in and I'll take you wherever you want to go. Where to?"

"I'm going to Asheville to get my sister out of jail."

"Ain't that lucky? I'm goin' there too!"

Already I'd figured out who she was. She and her sister were both hustlers around town. When we got to Enka Bridge, I pulled in there to go through West Asheville.

"How come you're goin' this way, mister?"

"So's we can git in some lovin'. I sure do need some lovin'."

"That right? Well, I guess it's O.K."

I had turned out the dash lights because I didn't want her to know who I was—for a half dozen reasons. I was in all the papers. A car passed us, and I turned my head so my face would be in shadow. It didn't work.

"Hey! I know you! I'd know those big brown eyes anywhere! Every cop in the State is looking for you!"

"You ready for some lovin'?" I asked her.

"Sure!"

We pulled off the highway, she yanked down her pants, and we got on with it. That girl had some mighty fine tail and knew

75

exactly what to do with it. I like my women with broad hips and nice big breasts, something you can get ahold of. That girl fit the bill to a tee.

I let her out at the edge of town and never did see her again, but I heard she was asking all over town for me, trying to catch up with me.

When I got home that time, Angie wasn't so cool. I stayed around for a while, pulling whatever jobs came along, doing O.K. One night the cops came and surrounded the house, yelling for me to come out. Of course, I didn't, so two of them came in.

I could have killed them both, but the outside was full of other police who had all kinds of guns. I hid my .38 so they wouldn't find it. Angie had just got home from work, so I told them I'd come out. I didn't want her to get hurt.

I stayed in jail about two weeks with the police on me every minute to tell them about the bakery holdup and the Malvern Hill Drug Store robbery. They showed me a statement from the guy that had escaped with me, telling about Angie cooking for us and bringing food and clothing while we were hiding at Thomas Wolfe's cabin.

"We'll get her for aiding and abetting if you don't come through, Frank!"

"Well, I did take the safe, but that's all."

One of their tricks was to put men in jail with me, pretending they were drunk, thinking they'd trap me into saying something about the bakery, but they never caught me. Solicitor Robert Swain told them they didn't have anything against me and might as well send me back to Central in Raleigh.

"We'll go over to Burnsville and check out with this Leroy. We picked him up and stuck him in there, you know."

I just laughed. "You won't get nothin' outa Leroy. He'll keep his trap shut. Leroy's a good boy."

I was dead wrong. Leroy sang like an opera star. Signed a statement against Clyde and me, got on the stand, and told everything he knew and twice as much he didn't know. It was fantastic. I didn't have a lawyer, and I sat there denying everything.

"You have anything to say, Mr. Watson?" the judge asked.

"I don't know nothin' about the whole mess, Your Honor. He's making it all up. Every word of it."

The jury went out and came back twice before they decided to give me five-to-ten for the safe job and ten years for the holdup, a total of twenty years, consecutively. Some of my friends beat hell out of Leroy later. He deserved every lick.

After a month at Central, they sent me to Albemarle Prison Camp. It's east of Charlotte in low mountains, the Uwharries. As soon as the boys got in from work that night, they asked me if I wanted to leave. I knew about all of them.

"Sure! I just got a new twenty year plan. You think I'm gonna sit in this rat's nest for twenty years?"

Saturday night we started cutting a hole through the roof of the toilet. We had to take turns standing watch against the finks and the hacks, the guards. We finished on Sunday night, but I had to show my knife to five or six men who had been too chicken to help cut the hole but were trying to crawl out through it ahead of us.

"Make your own hole, yellow bellies!"

The seven of us who had done all the work got through and up on the roof from which we were going to jump. A guard came around the corner, saw us, and started yelling. It didn't seem to occur to him to use his weapon.

"Come here and help me, you guys!" he was hollering. "The whole damn bunch is leaving! Going out through the toilet! Get out here and help me! Halt, you—"

We hit the fence and went over. I had been at that camp

exactly one week before I escaped. Some record! Two escapes in thirty days. A boy named Stringbean followed me. It was freezing cold all that night and the next day. We saw airplanes hunting for us, so we decided to get out of the area.

We got to a bridge, and Stringbean wanted to keep right on going across, but I stopped him. It's a good thing I did because right then a patrol car came along and picked up a guard that was hiding at the other end of the bridge. When anyone gets away, they always put guards on highway bridges, railway bridges, and little side roads. When it's dark, you can walk right up to one of those screws if you aren't careful.

When you're on the run, you need a cat's eyes, a dog's nose, and maybe a camel's stomach when water's scarce. A guardian angel might come in handy. I never knew any.

I got a pickup truck in front of a cotton mill, but we ran out of gas at Black Mountain Stone Quarry. It was raining pitchforks, but we walked over to the office of the quarry. The night watchman was sitting there reading, and his car was right outside the window. The place was lighted up bright as day. All he had to do was glance out the window, and he'd have seen us pushing the car.

We lit out for Asheville, and there I put the boy out. He was yellow, and I didn't need him. Angie wasn't especially surprised to see me when I came home for my .38 and some clothes.

I hooked up with a fellow I'd done time with, and we were going to hold up the Bolling Chair Factory in Swannanoa to get its safe with a payroll. I didn't have any luck finding the safe, so I went to sleep in the car I'd just stolen in Asheville.

In the middle of the night, I woke up and saw flashlights everywhere and a lot of people milling around. I knew I was done for. Come to find out, they were raiding some colored people nearby. A close one.

The next night, when I went home, my stepson's wife met me at the door. She told me to come on in; he'd be back in a couple of minutes. What she didn't tell me was that two detectives, Parker and Maney, were hiding in the house. They had told her that they'd see that she and Angie both did some time if they warned me.

I smelled trouble. I pulled my gun just as Parker came into the kitchen from the living room.

"Don't move, Parker, or you're dead," I said, waving the gun in his face. I started backing toward the door when Maney jumped me and jammed his pistol into my side.

"Drop the gun, Frank," Maney said, cold as steel. I tried to throw him off, but I couldn't, so I let down the hammer on my .38 and threw it on the floor. Maney couldn't shoot me without me shooting Parker. Later they gave Maney a commendation for saving Parker's life and moved him up to Detective Sergeant.

Back to Central Prison to wait for them to decide what to do with me this time. First they hauled me and the other boys back to Albemarle for a trial for escaping. We broke the back door on the dog wagon, planning to jump out, but some people in a car behind us warned the driver, and he slammed on his brakes so we piled up in a heap. The guards handcuffed us all together and took us on to Central again.

Well, at least in the lockup I could do some reading. The *Upper Room* and the Gideon Bible were all that was at hand when we were in the hole, but I finally began to read just to pass the time. Better than sitting there.

10

THOSE GUYS ON THE PRISON BOARD WERE A HARD-EYED LOT. THAT
was why they were on the prison board. But then I was no
dove myself. I'd been locked up for seven months before I
faced them.

"You know what's ahead, don't you, Watson?"

I didn't say anything.

"As soon as we get Ivy Bluff ready, you'll be there for a
year at least. You know about Ivy Bluff?"

"A little."

"What have you got to say about Ivy?"

"So? It's Ivy Bluff."

"We're mighty proud of the place, Watson, Little Alcatraz,
they tell us. A model for every hard-core prison in the U.S.A.
Completely escape-proof. When you get in there, that's it.
Until you straighten up."

"Yeah."

"You got anything more to say?"

What do you say to people like that? I just looked at them.
Long before we ever laid eyes on the place, three of us were
planning to escape.

All we were allowed to have was a comb, a toothbrush, and
toothpaste. Period. No radio, no TV, no books, no reading
matter of any kind, not even a newspaper or a Bible.

Red Eye Meadows met us at the gate. "You guys been sent
here to git killed. Any of you gits out of line, you're dead."

Our first sight of the place had told us that anyway. Ivy

80

Bluff's main building was T-shaped, with offices and dormitories to the front, the mess hall and kitchen to the rear. The lockup and sick bay were over the kitchen. Each side of the T had two dormitories, each with about twenty beds. The beds were solid steel with the legs sunk in the concrete floor so they couldn't be moved or torn apart and used as weapons. The sinks, commodes, and showers were built so they couldn't be torn from the wall and destroyed.

The prison sat on a high cliff above the Tar River, with guard towers on all four corners. The guards, all dead shots, had binoculars and .30-.30 rifles. When we first went in, the building smelled of paint, cement, and disinfectant because it was still so new. Outside, the ground was still North Carolina red clay—no grass, only a couple of trees.

The rock hole at Ivy Bluff had been dynamited out of a mountain facing the river. We used a wagon drill for making holes in the floor of the rock; then they would pack those holes with dynamite and blow boulders loose for us to break up with sixteen-pound sledges. We worked there ten hours a day in the broiling sun—not much help in trying to develop a good attitude.

They always fed us real good. They had to because they worked hell out of us at the rock hole; then on weekends they had us spading up the yard so they could plant grass seed. Ivy Bluff was a good place for quiet meditation. Nothing to do but think when you weren't working.

Whoever built the prison had thrown some hacksaw blades down in the dirt, and they got covered with trash. Funny how my rake dug one up, nearly new. I told the guys to gather round me so the hacks in the gun tower wouldn't see what I was going to do. Then I broke it in two and stuck it in my shoe.

The routine at Ivy Bluff was set up so we stripped off when

we went to work, put our clothes on a bed, went through a shakedown, and came into a room where our work clothes were. At night, the same thing in reverse. Take off our work clothes, another shakedown, into the cell block, shower and wait for supper.

I got the hacksaw blades from my shoe, slipped them into my glove, threw the gloves into a corner. If they were found, no one would get into trouble. Next morning they were still there. At the rock hole I tried them out to see if they'd cut drill steel. They did, real good. I put grease on them so they wouldn't rust and hid them.

A couple of my friends started working on me, said no one could get out of Ivy Bluff. I'd get killed, sure as hell. I listened. I had nothing to lose. I'd make a try.

George and Roy joined me. We thought the punishment hole was the weakest point, so we decided to break some of their rules and get put in there. We'd have to grease the hacksaw blades and hide them up one of our tails, the one place they didn't search. Nobody wanted the job, but it was the only way. George drew the short straw, so he put the blades up his ass, cussed out the foreman, and went to the hole.

The next day Roy and I bucked work. When everyone else trudged out to the truck, we just sat there. Red Eye came around.

"What's up, Watson? Feelin' porely this mornin'?"

"I ain't workin' for you no more, Cap'n Meadows."

"Watson, if you'll just get off your can and go to work peaceful, I'll forget it."

He made a move toward his weapon. I could see that ugly color coming up in his eye. If he killed me, I'd never get to prove to him that I could get out of his safe deposit box. He clapped us in the hole.

One of my buddies named Bill, who had been put in the

hole for cursing, gave me $120 he had smuggled in. No place to spend it, so he gave it to me for escape money. I heard one of the guards say they'd let him out of the hole if he'd ask, so when I got there I told him he could go with us if he wanted to. He said no, he didn't want to get killed.

"You could do us a favor by gettin' outta here and gettin' a guy to play sick so they put him in the hole with George."

"I get it. George has the blades. Well, I can try."

We were there two weeks, starving, mad, ready to give up and try again later, when they brought in another boy. He had the blades! As soon as the guards were gone, I slid my blanket along the floor at the bottom of the barred door. The boy threw the blades on it, and I pulled them into my cell. We were in business!

I started right away to saw the bars at the bottom of the door. The screws couldn't see a cut unless they got down and looked, and they weren't expecting anything like that anyway. When I finished with mine, I tossed the blades to Roy; then he sawed out and passed them on. I was to go first, then help them.

We went into the hole around the first of November, 1956. It was now Thanksgiving, a year after my escape from Lincolnton. As an extra dose of cruelty, the guards would come in and pick their teeth and tell us juicy details of what they had had to eat and what was to be served for Thanksgiving. It tore up the other guys, who were starving too, but I told them not to worry. Those cats weren't going to have any big Thanksgiving feast. They'd be out on the roads hunting us.

I hadn't figured on how tough the bars would be to bend. They were case-hardened steel. I had to use every bit of muscle I had left after three or four weeks' starvation in the hole. One of the boys was watching for the guard and whispered that he was coming about the time I got mine bent part way.

"Get up to your doors, all of you," I whispered to them. "If he sees all of us up so close, he won't think to look down."

The guard saw we were all accounted for, turned around and left.

I started again trying to bend those damn bars. My hands got big sores from it, but I finally made it so I could get through. I've got a 52-inch chest, so that makes some problems.

I went to get out the boy in the cell across from me. I could bend his bars only a little. I was pooped, so I went into our little shower room and broke out a piece of pipe to use as a lever. It was made of lead, and I split it apart.

"Hurry!" Roy told me. "It's almost time for the guard to come back!"

"I am, damn it! Now see if you can make it!" I was grunting and tugging until he got his head and shoulders through, but his damn hips were too thick. "Get your clothes off! I had to take mine off. Didn't take but two shakes to get 'em back on again. Now! Put your arms through here. *Suck in!*" I grabbed his arms and ran backwards as hard as I could. I dragged him through those steel bars and left pieces of his skin stuck on them. "Get dressed!"

One more guy. He hadn't been in the hole as long as we had, so he hadn't lost any weight, and he hadn't sawed as many bars either. I did everything I could to get him out. I sawed; I pulled; I cussed.

"The guard! Here he comes!"

I was planning to turn loose everyone on Ivy Bluff. It didn't look good.

There was a solid steel door to the outside. I got my ear right up against it so I could hear the guard. It was raining like hell, making it hard for me to tell one sound from another. I heard him put his key in the lock. I let him get the door opened about a foot; then I ran against it so it hit the guard and spun him halfway around. I thought his gun was in the holster under his coat, but it was in his hand all the time. I grabbed him around the waist, picked him up so I could throw him on the floor. He tried to shoot me, but he missed and hit Roy in the hip. I didn't know it then.

By then I had the guard face down. I got hold of the barrel of his gun and held it against his side. I hit him on the jaw and twisted the gun over his wrist so I broke his trigger finger; then I knocked him out with his own gun.

He'd already fired four shots. The guards' sleeping quarters were right outside the fence, so the shots woke them up. On came the big floodlights. The whole camp was lit up like a Christmas tree, and there was yelling and running and all kinds of noise.

I told the other guy I was sorry that I'd have to leave him, but if I didn't we'd all be killed.

"It's O.K. Get movin'!"

I headed for the fence. Then I heard Roy screaming. "Don't leave me, Frank! Don't leave me! I been hit!" If I'd known that, I might have killed the damn guard.

"I won't leave you!" I ran back, put his arm around my neck and started dragging him. I got him over the fence and dropped him down; then I went over. Somehow I got him over the second fence too. The lights made it easy to see where we were going, and there was a hell of a lot of confusion, yelling, running, banging on things.

The creek down below was shoulder deep from the rain, some places flooding over its banks, but I hauled that kid across it, holding his head out of that icy water and wondering when my foot might slip and we'd both get drowned. I was getting weaker by the minute, but I couldn't quit and I couldn't desert the kid. We got into the woods, took a couple of breaths, and went on.

I pulled him through an open field, then across a little dirt road and into some more woods. I dropped him down and thought we could rest, but a car stopped and let a guard out.

"We gotta keep movin', kid. Hang on!"

We moved across another road and flopped down behind some brush. Another car, another guard let out, poking around, gun cocked, sloshing through the mud and wet bushes. Finally I heard him tromping off the other way.

It was bitter cold. We didn't have any shoes; we'd lost them in the creek. We were soaked, me in stripes, Roy in brown clothes.

That kid didn't make a sound. I knew he was in pretty bad shape. The bullet had gone clear through his leg and come out under the cheek of his ass.

"Frank? Did you kill that guard?"

"Which one? I'd like to get 'em all." I tried to act kind of easy and tough so he wouldn't feel any worse.

"The one inside, the one you slugged."

"Who cares?"

"Nobody."

"That's right, kid."

Roy didn't live to be old. His own daddy killed him in a drinking spree.

We kept going, traveling at night, hiding by day, me trying to take care of him as best I could. He never once whined, but he was in terrible bad shape. I had the .38 I'd taken from the guard. I was so damn bitter I could have killed a hundred of them and enjoyed it.

I got Roy to an old abandoned barn and found some gunnysacks to put over him. He was bad off and suffering like hell, but he never said one word about it. Pure guts.

The guards were running up and down the roads like ants: the State Patrol, the Sheriff's Department, even some of the men from Central Prison. The whole county was in an uproar.

Raleigh *News and Observer*, Nov. 23, 1956

Two convicts overpowered a guard at Ivy Bluff close security prison in Caswell County Wednesday night, scaled two fences and escaped. State Prisons Director William F. Bailey said a search was underway for the two.

Bailey identified the two as Roy Anderson, 21, of Wilkes County, serving a total of 40 years for burglary, robbery and larceny, and Frank Watson, 34, of Buncombe County, serving 20 years for burglary, robbery and larceny.

The two men were confined in separate cells in the new prison's segregation unit for punishment, Bailey explained, and a guard was supposed to check the segregation cells every hour.

Around midnight a guard entered the building for a check. The two had managed to get out of their cells and charged the guard when he opened the door. They knocked him down.

During the scuffle, the guard fired his gun three times. Bailey explained he was apparently trying to empty the weapon to prevent the prisoners being armed if they escaped.

The Ivy Bluff prison was opened last July. The escape was its first. The prison is located near Youngsville.

11

THAT NIGHT WE BROKE INTO A HOUSE. THE PEOPLE RAN A STORE right next to it, and they were all there working. We found some clothes, matches, a double-barreled shotgun, a box of shells, some money—but not one bite to eat. They must have brought whatever they needed home from the store. I had hauled the boy in with me, as much to get warm as anything. We fell across a bed exhausted. We watched the store from the bedroom window so we'd know what was going on.

A carload of cops drove up. A couple of them jumped out and started talking to the man at the store.

"We'll get the people when they come home," I told Roy. "They'll have the money with them from the cash box. And they've sent the cops away because of course they don't know anything."

Here came the woman and her daughter. I stepped out with the .38. "Keep it quiet and you'll be O.K.," I told them, but they screamed like hell and ran out. I didn't want to shoot.

"Come on! We gotta get the hell outa here! Hang on!" We got out the back door, circled around to the highway and here came the Highway Patrol and the Sheriff's Department. I dragged the boy across the road, threw him into a ditch, and jumped in after him. The ditch was eight or ten feet deep and full of blackberry bushes.

"Are you hurt, Frank? Are you hurt?"

"No, but I tore my new overcoat."

"You got the guns?"

"Yeah."

"Shells too?"

"Yup."

It was dark as pitch and you could see a car a long ways, so we'd gotten across the road O.K. We crawled along the ditch for a mile or so, and here came another load of screws. We flattened down again. The car stopped and backed up into a little side road, right across from where I lay with the shotgun on them. I could have got them all. After a while they pulled out.

It was almost daylight, so we stumbled back into the woods. At Ivy Bluff they shave your head, so you can imagine how we looked. Sunken eyes, skin and bones, thirty pounds lighter than usual, beards, filth, hunger, dried blood, stink. We'd both nearly frozen our feet in that creek. We looked like hell.

No food that day either. We had to drink creek water. About dusk we started out again.

"Roy, we gotta eat."

"Why don't you leave me, Frank? You can make it alone."

"Whattaya think I am, some kind of animal?"

"We're livin' like animals, ain't we?"

"I'll find something, kid. Just hold on."

We came to a house right next to the woods with a refrigerator on the back porch. The people that lived there were moving around inside. With the .38 in my hand, I eased the door of the icebox open and got six pounds of bacon and four quarts of milk. For most of my life, I figured a .38 was the best friend I'd ever have.

We moved back into the woods and found a dry place under a creek bank. I built us a fire, broke some long sticks to hold the bacon, and leaned against a tree trunk to enjoy that heavenly smell. We drank down the milk while the meat was cooking. After we'd stuffed ourselves, I tore off my shirttail, dipped it in the bacon grease, and cleaned the gun.

"Now we can move on, kid, with that grub in us. How's your leg?"

"Not bad at all. Doin' fine."

"I'll get you to a doctor, once we're free of those hacks."

"Forget it! I'm O.K."

We got to a store that had a garage behind it. There was a 1948 Ford. It sure had a hot motor. We wired it up, opened the garage doors, and I took off down the driveway to the street, sideswiping a new car that sat there. The people ran out of the store, but I kept right on going.

Out of town a ways the lights went out, so I pulled in behind a country schoolhouse to work on them. The State Patrol went racing by, looking for us.

We spotted a drive-in place, and I asked the girl for eight hamburgers and two thick malteds.

"You-all must be plumb starved!" she said, kind of giggling. "Eight burgers for two people!"

"You didn't miss it far, baby!" I said, real polite.

When we'd wolfed down the food, we got to a motel in Winston-Salem, took a bath, shaved, and went to sleep. We told the man at the desk that we'd been on a hunting trip in the mountains and that's why we looked so crummy. He didn't seem to give a damn *what* we'd been doing, long as he got his dough.

Next morning at Sears Roebuck we got some clothes and shoes and headed for Roy's home town, North Wilkesboro. He knew where we could get a safe, so after we hid in the woods all day, we broke in. Between us we got that 500-pound safe rolled onto a pickup truck parked in back, Roy dragging his leg but never once mentioning it. I wired the engine and off we went, way out into the country. There wasn't much money in it, but we decided to hole up for a couple of weeks since the area looked pretty quiet and Roy needed to take it easy.

Near Christmas we headed toward Princeton, West Virginia, to find a place to rob. We were driving a 1952 Olds that really rolled. We stopped at a high school outside of town, and I broke in.

"What's going on? *Who are you?*" I jumped a foot when a night watchman threw a flashlight over Roy. "One move and I'll shoot! I got a shotgun, kid, and I'll use it! Git! No funny stuff! *Out!* Hear?"

He hadn't seen me, so I eased along behind them. When we got outdoors, I stuck the .38 in his ribs, reached over his shoulder for the flashlight, and slammed him up against the wall.

"Don't hurt me, mister! Don't hurt me! I'm an old man—"

"Shut up!" I got his wallet and tossed it to Roy.

Another pickup was sitting there. I didn't know there was a man in it until he hopped out and ran.

"Get the car, Roy! Quick! That guy's goin' for the law!"

He didn't drive too good, so I grabbed the wheel and we took off. We came over the hill into Princeton straight into a Highway Patrol roadblock. A couple of cars were ahead of us, so I slowed down. When the Patrol opened up to let them through, I poured the gas to the Olds and nearly ran down a couple of patrolmen.

The highway runs right through Princeton's main street, and damn if there wasn't some kind of Christmas parade blocking traffic; lots of kids on the sidewalk, bright lights, bands, the works.

A patrol car fell in behind us, so I took off up a side street. Dead end. I turned around in a yard and spun back the same way, the patrol car right on my tail. I couldn't go through town or back through the roadblock, so I tried another side street. *Dead end.*

"When I stop, you run! Jump as far as you can, and then beat it!"

I'd kept the door on my side open, so I hit the brakes, slid out, and ran between two houses. I didn't have time to notice what Roy was doing. A patrolman shot at me five times. The paper said I'd been hit and they'd found blood on the ground. One shot had hit me in the leg and had barely broken the skin. Really nothing.

Roy's leg was healed up enough that he could get along O.K. by himself, but the hell of it was that he had all the money. I didn't have one red cent.

I hid out until I figured they had stopped looking for me; then I tried to find Roy. I spent two hours, mingling with the crowds who were watching the parade and doing Christmas shopping, but I was really hunting for the boy. No luck. Much later I found out they'd nabbed him, still in the front seat.

I kept on walking to the other edge of town and stole a car. I had to find one with a full tank because I didn't have any money. It was late at night when I ran out of gas out in the country on my way back into North Carolina. I sat in the car, freezing. About 4:30 or 5:00 in the morning, a newspaper delivery man came along and stopped, so I asked him if he'd take me into the next town so I could get some gas. When I got out of the car, I thanked him, walked down the street out of sight, and stole another car.

At daylight I pulled into the woods on a little side road and hid out all day. By nighttime I was in Charlotte, so I could hold up a supermarket. I got enough cash that I didn't need to heist a bank.

Don't hold up a bank unless you're plumb at the end of your rope. Too much heat from the F.B.I. I know a lot of bank robbers, and they all say the same thing: a heap of money, a heap of trouble, and a heap of prison time. When they say, "Time is one thing I have a heap of!" I don't laugh. What's so damn funny about doing time?

With the money I got in Charlotte, I was safe for a while, so I went to Asheville to a friend's house.

"Hi, Frank," he said when he saw me. "I been expectin' ya."

"How come? Mind reader?"

"Don't ya see the papers?"

"I don't have no time to read the papers," I said, sort of easy, but I knew damn well what he was talking about.

"Here you are, man, spread all over the front page. Looks like you're trying to make yourself quite a hero. Who you think you are? Robin Hood? No, couldn't be Robin Hood. He helped the poor. Houdini? Yeah, more like Houdini, escape artist. How about Jesse James? That's the boy, ol' Jesse."

He handed me a copy of the Asheville paper. "Some chance they'll be watchin' this house too, Frank, you know. I'm not exactly real tickled to see you. I guess I won't turn you out, but—well—"

I didn't pay any attention to him, just started reading.

Handsome [handsome!] Frank Watson, an Asheville prison escape artist believed to be the man behind a service station holdup near here and possibly the brains [brains!] behind two Asheville safe thefts, yesterday was declared an Outlaw—

"That's what they're callin' ya, Frank. An *Outlaw*."

—and officers were told to shoot him down if he resists arrest. Watson, 34, who bolted the "escape-proof" Ivy Bluff prison camp in Caswell county the day before Thanksgiving, is thought to be holed up somewhere in Buncombe County.

"They got quite a list of things against you, Frank."

"Yeah. Guess I won't bother to read 'em all. I know the list better'n they do." I put down the paper and slid back in the chair, trying to relax. "Got any coffee?"

"Might. Did you read the whole story? That about the F.B.I.?"

"No, I didn't see that. They want me to work for them?"

"Not quite. They want to nail your hide to the wall. You're on their Ten Most Wanted, Frank. That's bad."

12

IT SEEMED LIKE A GOOD IDEA TO HEAD WEST. I DROVE THE OLDS to a car lot near the oil company I was planning to rob, picked out a new Ford, broke into the office and got the keys for it, and put all my things—I didn't have much—into the trunk. I made a mask out of a pillowcase I'd gotten from my buddy's sister, drove the Olds over to the oil company he'd fingered for me as the price for getting me out of the house, and at about two in the morning, I walked around to the back where there was a storeroom. The manager of the place showed up, so I put on my pillowcase mask, stuck some pebbles in my mouth so my voice would sound funny, pulled my .38, and waited in the doorway until he turned around.

"Hold it!" I took his flashlight, frisked him, and took his gun and money, put my arm around his waist and the pistol under his chin so I could walk him to where I'd left the car.

"Don't shoot! Don't shoot! I'll do whatever you want!"

"Shut your trap!" I hardly recognized my own voice.

"I just got married. Don't hurt me!"

"Congratulations!" I said to him. "I hope you have a long and happy life. You can get back to your wife if you do what I say."

"Anything! Anything!"

I shoved him down into a ditch. "Don't you make a move! And don't yell! Got it?"

"I hear you. I'll—"

I drove a block away, hid the Olds under a bridge, walked

back over the bridge, and hid near the lot where the new Ford was. Here came the cops buzzing around, looking everywhere, up and down the road like hornets.

When they got tired, I drove away in the Ford. The money wasn't much. Hardly worth the effort. The car needed gas, so I started to pull into a truck stop. There was a State patrolman, so I had to go on, and, of course, ran out near Morganton. Some kids came along in a car, so I gave them five bucks to bring me some gas, and I went rolling along.

Copper Hill, Chattanooga—I felt great. There's nothing in the world like feeling so free. No domestic worries, no one to be responsible for, a good car under you, some dough in your pockets, no strings except that Outlaw stuff, and I'd gotten around that. Jesse James should have had it so good.

My birthday and Christmas had come and gone without any notice. The best meal of the year in prison is always on Christmas Day, and I'd never had a birthday present in my whole life, so all I'd really missed was some turkey and cranberries.

In Arkansas a couple of hitchhikers rode with me a while. They were just off the chain gang. They started telling me all sorts of exciting stuff about a fellow who had broken out of Ivy Bluff and was still on the loose.

"Supposed to be escape-proof! Little Alcatraz, they call it. Some guy! Sawed bars, climbed fences, got another guy out with him after the guy'd been shot!"

"Quite a man, you think?"

"Right! I'd sure like to be with him!"

"You think they'll ever catch a guy like that?"

"They ain't yet!"

It was a great trip. I put those hitchhikers out in Little Rock, went on to Fort Smith, robbed a store there, and then on through the good old Cookston Hills to Muskogee, Oklahoma, and Oklahoma City. I got some more money there and picked up a boy who wanted to work in the oil fields in New Mexico.

Just outside Tucumcari, an old man and two girls in a new Plymouth came by and wanted to race. We took off, side by side. In no time the city police stopped us.

I didn't have a license or any kind of I.D. I did have a gun where I could get to it, but I hoped I wouldn't have to use it.

"Sorry I was going so fast, officer," I said, real polite. "First new car I've had in quite a spell, and it sort of runs away with me." I was telling the truth, of course, and he seemed to think so too, so he let me go with a warning.

"Better watch it when you get out to the edge of town," he told me. "The State Patrol is on the prowl out there."

"Thanks a lot, officer. I'll be extra careful."

He touched his cap and off we went.

In Farmington, New Mexico, I got a job driving a tractor-trailer. Good money and long hours. At least $200 a week. I met a girl named Rose at a cafe where I ate, and we liked each other a lot. I was some kind of lonesome. That's one thing about being on the run. It's lonesome.

Angie and I had called it quits, and she was divorcing me, so I moved in with Rose and her four kids. They thought as much of me as if I'd been their father. Funny, lots of people on the outside liked me; why couldn't I make it out there? I always blew it.

One day when I was in the cafe eating lunch a man kept looking at me, so I asked the waitress who he was, and she said, "He's an F.B.I. man. He eats here every once in a while. They're always around looking for someone on the Wanted List."

Rose had been wanting to go visit her folks in Sterling, Colorado, so we bought a new 40-foot house trailer and had it put in her folks' back yard there. I got a job on a bulldozer clearing

97

land for ranchers. One day her mother called me into the kitchen and handed me ten $100 bills. I was startled.

"What's this for?"

"It's your wedding present, John. My daughter told us you'd had just a quiet wedding ceremony at a Jaypee's, but she's so happy being Mrs. John Masterson and the kids are so happy with their new father that we wanted to—well, we're glad to have you as a part of our family, John." And she kissed me on the cheek.

"I—I can't take this!" I protested. She finally insisted, and when I told Rose, she said, "Forget it. They've got plenty of money, and it makes them feel good to give some to you."

"But we're not married, honey! And I'm makin' good dough—"

"Forget it!" she said again. "If my folks want to give John Kitson Masterson something, take it and enjoy it." It sounded funny, her using the name I'd given myself.

That time was one of the good things in my life. When the bulldozing job was finished, I hauled oil field drill stem casing pipe and helped move oil drills from one place to another and set them up. I was making good money, honest money, and I didn't need to rob anyone. Her kids loved me and made a big fuss over me, and she was a plenty good woman, any way you wanted it, believe me. If it hadn't been for the law, I'd have been set for life.

We didn't work when it was raining because the mud got too deep, so I was home reading some Zane Grey books I'd gotten from the library when someone came to the door.

"Answer it, honey," I told her. "It's probably some insurance salesman. Tell him we don't want any."

Sure enough, I'd guessed right. He asked her where I worked and whether she thought we had enough insurance, what with four kids and all. Now I know he was an F.B.I. man, but I didn't know it then. He must have heard what I said and picked it up for his own purposes. He should have heard what I said after I found out the truth.

Two weeks later five of us loaded up our trucks with drill casings and headed north for Aggerson, Wyoming. I was driving a big Super White Tractor with a two-way radio like the others so we could reach each other if we needed help. We always gassed up at a certain filling station in Cheyenne, Wyoming. I was the last in line. There were men going around poking their noses up under the trucks as well as looking at the loads we were carrying.

"What are those cats after?" I asked the Pusher, which is what they call a boss in the oil field. "Looking for gold?"

"Probably I.C.C. men," he said comfortably. "They check us out now and then, watching for overweight, not enough sleep hours and all that jazz."

When my turn came, I pulled up by the pump, not worried because I had an I.D. card and driver's permit. I got out of the cab and started putting on my coat because it was cold. I felt a gun in my back.

"Put your hands up, Watson. F.B.I."

"You got the wrong man," I said. "My name is Masterson. I guess it does sound something like Watson. John K. Masterson. Here, look at my I.D. And this is my driver's permit."

"Looks O.K. Now let me see your left arm." I rolled up my sleeve.

"H'm," he said, frowning. "You're supposed to have a tattoo on your left arm. I don't see one."

Right then the Pusher came over. "Listen, I don't know who you're looking for, but you've got the wrong man. Masterson is one of our long-time drivers. How about just knocking it off? We've got a load of drills to deliver."

I didn't dare look at the boss. He knew as well as I did that

99

I'd only worked for them a month. We were going to beat them out!

"Sorry," the F.B.I. man said. "These things happen, you know. We don't like to take chances."

I started to get back in the cab, but the second fellow came up. "What say we take him to town and fingerprint him anyway? It won't take long. I have a gut feeling that we might be right. What'd you say your name was?"

"Masterson. John Kitson Masterson. Here's my I.D."

They took me into Cheyenne to jail anyway and inked my fingers. Then they got on the radio.

"He's Watson all right," one said to the other. "All right, Watson, let me see your right arm. I think they made a little mistake on your records. Yup, here's the tattoo. *Right* arm. Says 'Franky.' Kind of sweet, isn't it?"

"Sweet, hell," I said. "So ya got me. What now?"

"Jail for a while. One phone call. We'll turn you over to the U.S. Marshal to waive jurisdiction, unless you want to sweat out a lost cause."

"Why bother?"

"That's the way I'd figure too, Watson."

I called Rose and gave her the word. She and her folks and kids started crying and carrying on and saying they couldn't believe I was an outlaw from North Carolina. I'd been so good to her and her children, and they all loved me so much. I had to act real tough so I wouldn't be doing the same thing, bawling like a baby. I always figured that if I ever let myself cry or even squeeze out a few tears it meant that I was going crazy. That's true; I really believed that.

"Could you bring me my shaving stuff and some clean clothes?" I asked matter-of-factly. "I need them."

The U.S. Marshals arrived at the jail bright and early the next morning. My clothes and shaving stuff weren't there yet, and I tried to get them to wait.

"Not on your life, Watson. That girl would be helping you get away, and the first thing we know we'd have lost our pigeon. The government's got plenty of clothes for you. Any size you need. Even your size. All the same color, however, but it's one that you wear a lot. Masterson, huh? Bat, maybe? They made a movie about Bat Masterson, didn't they? Kitson —oh, I get it! Kit Carson? What are you, Watson, a hero-worshiper?"

As we went through town I looked over at the Stockman's Hotel, and there was my car sitting in front. I knew I'd never see Rose or my new family again. A man has to have a family.

On the trip east they were right nice to me. I could have anything I wanted to eat, although I was locked up for the night. At Dodge City they asked me if I wanted to see Boot Hill. I was clanking along in chains, but of course I wanted to go. Not a very romantic spot, believe me. Gave me the shivers.

That night they locked me in their death cell there, and a nice young man came to see me.

"I'm the 36th sheriff here since Wyatt Earp," he told me. "The job's different now. Lot of routine—drunks, knifings, petty thievery."

"No real outlaws?" I asked, trying to be friendly.

"You. One at a time is enough. Say, did you kill a guard when you skipped at North Carolina's Little Alcatraz?"

"I don't think so. I never killed anyone."

"The Marshal said you did. I'll get some clean sheets, and my wife will fix you some supper. She's a great cook."

"Some of mine were too," I said. "Tell her not too much salt."

"Want something to read?" he asked, picking up some books from a table. "Here's a paperback Hemingway."

"Which one? I've read most of his stuff. Good man."

"This one's short stories. You might like the one called 'The Killers.'"

Asheville *Citizen-Times*, May 25, 1957

Outlaw Frank Watson will be returned Friday to Asheville, the scene of many of his scrapes with the law.

Federal authorities will bring him here from Cheyenne, Wyoming, where he was captured last Friday.

He will be tried in U.S. District Court on three charges of automobile theft and unlawful flight to avoid prosecution. . . .

Watson, 36, also is wanted by State authorities. He escaped from a maximum security state prison camp last November while serving a 15–20 year term for the armed robbery of a grocery store.

It was his fourth such escape from a prison camp. . . .

If they were going to print so much about me in the papers all the time, why couldn't they get my age right? I wasn't thirty-six, wouldn't be until December.

13

Next day on the way to Fort Smith, we stopped for gas, and a man at the station looked in and saw me in handcuffs.

"Got him hog-tied, huh, Marshal?"

"Yeah. Have to, some of 'em."

"Coupla weeks ago two guys tried to hold me up, so me and my pet bulldog, we got 'em."

"Really?"

"Yes siree! My dog done got the gun away from one, and the other 'un run!" He started chuckling at how smart he was.

I was already mad and bitter enough, so I spit out at him, "Listen, if one of them guys had been me, you *and* your shittin' dog woulda bin fodder for the undertaker."

The Marshal glared at him and muttered something about keeping his big mouth shut and me keeping mine buttoned too, and we left—I guess he knew he had a kind of volcano on his hands.

We got into Fort Smith that night. It wouldn't have surprised me one bit to see a gallows with my name on it. Local people knew me, and the cops gathered around to look over the catch. I'd whipped a couple of them good when we were kids, and they hadn't forgotten it. They didn't say much, but I knew exactly what they were thinking. By the time we pulled out early the next morning, they probably weren't talking about anything else but Ol' Frankie Watson finally makin' it to the Top Ten. I hated their guts.

One of the crummiest jails I was ever in was in Chattanooga,

103

Tennessee. The jailer was just as crummy as the jail. Next morning I heard him asking the other prisoners if I'd bothered any of them, so I yelled at him, "Hell, yes! I kicked the be-Jesus out of every fucking punk in this fucking jail. Come on over where I can reach you and I'll do the same to you, you bastard!"

When the Marshal heard about it, he just laughed, but I imagined he would be damn glad to get me off his hands. When we stopped outside Asheville to get a malted milk, the Marshal went to a phone booth to call his office, leaving me in the car with the Deputy Marshal.

People were staring at us out of the window of the drive-in, and pretty soon two carloads of state troopers drove up, jumped out real fast, and raced over to the car with their guns drawn. When they looked in, they saw the cuffs and leg irons.

"What's up, men?" the Marshal asked, real easy, as he came back. "Hunting someone?"

"Thought we'd make an arrest," a couple of them said sheepishly.

"You must think you know this guy! We've had a nice long trip together, him and me."

"Everyone knows Frank Watson! Every police officer in four states has his picture!" And they all pulled out photographs of me to show him.

"These gentlemen are worried about me, Frank," the Marshal said. "They seem to think I may have a problem getting you to the Marshal's office in Asheville. Must be all of six or seven miles. When I called in, the office deputy wanted to know if I still had you."

I laughed.

"These patrolmen want to make a big show of helping me escort you to jail. What say, Frank?"

"I know the way to jail."

When we got there, the whole Sheriff's Department was lined up out front, like a crowd waiting for the Queen of England.

"Where'ya bin, Frank? We bin missin' ya!"

"Down in Mexico, holdin' up trains. Had a great time."

They locked me up on the Federal side in the middle cell, with no one else on that side and no one allowed to see me but law officers. Angie wouldn't be coming anyway because she'd been serving time up in Alderson, West Virginia, in the Federal Women's Prison for taking hacksaw blades to her son while he was in jail.

When I broke out at Ivy Bluff, they said the whole prison there was ringed with lawmen, figuring I'd try to get to her.

The F.B.I. came around, proper and legal-acting as hell. "Mr. Watson, you have been declared an Outlaw by the State of North Carolina, and the Federal Bureau of Investigation has placed you on its list of the Ten Most Wanted Men. Did you know this? We must advise you of your right to remain silent, your right to counsel, and also that anything you say may be held against you. Now, Mr. Watson, if you will cooperate with us—"

"Why?"

"If you will cooperate with us, your sentence might not be for more than five years if we can get all the charges tried in one court."

I hadn't seen a lawyer yet, but I knew they had me on three of the cars I stole and the guard's gun. Five years would be a damn sight better than fifteen or twenty. And it wasn't going to be quite as easy to break out any more. Not that the other times were exactly what you'd call easy.

"O.K."

Judge Wilson Warlick heard my case. They appointed I. C. Crawford as my attorney, but I never saw him until I went into the courtroom. He came over and asked me what they had me for!

"Why don't you read the papers?" I asked.

The judge sentenced me to eighteen years at Atlanta Federal Penitentiary. "Mr. Watson, do you have anything to say?"

"You gave me too much time, Judge."

The F.B.I. denied ever making me that offer of five years for cooperating with them. The judge said the F.B.I. would never do a thing like *that*, not those nice guys. It was my word against theirs.

"I never cry over spilled milk, Judge."

I sat there and took it, head-on. Next stop, Atlanta.

They handcuffed and leg-ironed me and locked my shoes in the trunk of the car. If I escaped, I'd be barefooted. When we got there, they gave me back my shoes and let me put them on.

I still had the beautiful Longines wrist watch and a nice ring with my name inside that Rose gave me.

"Where you want these things sent, Watson? You can't keep 'em here, you know. Too many thieves around."

"Was that supposed to be a joke?" I growled. "Send them to my girl. Here's her address. Be sure the stuff is insured. It's worth a damn lot. And these are the keys to her car."

"Mighty nice stuff. Cost a pretty penny," one of the guards kept saying. I said to myself, I'll bet that's the last time anyone sees them. It was. Rose never got them. I began raising hell about it and made them check it out. The word finally came back that the package had been lost in the mail.

That's when I really blew my stack. They finally scrounged up fifty bucks so I'd shut up. I watched every damn screw in the prison to try to catch someone wearing my watch and my ring, but I never did. I would have gone up the side of his jaw if I'd found them, believe me.

Not all the crooks are locked up, that's for sure.

Naturally, the first thing I did when I got to Atlanta in 1958 was to look for a place to break out. They were building a new laundry and dormitory, and they had built a wooden toilet over the manhole so the construction workers could take a crap there. The water from the washing machines in the old laundry went through a pipe into the manhole and then out to a creek behind the penitentiary. I had already figured that the only way to get out of that place was to dig a tunnel. The problem with a tunnel is that you have to have a way to get rid of the dirt.

When I inspected the manhole on the sly, I found that it was about twenty feet from the wall, right under a guard tower. The toilet inside was country style with three holes. I had to find a way to get down the manhole without the guards knowing it, so I built a trap door that could be lifted and put back quickly.

All the troublemakers there were put on the construction gang, so I got into a fight on purpose and was put on the gang. My plan was working fine.

The walls below the manhole were of brick and cement with an iron ladder so you could go up and down. The plan was to break a hole through that brick wall and dig a tunnel under the outside wall. To do that I needed tools.

The tools used by the construction boys were counted every night by the construction foreman, so if I took a tool I'd have to replace it before the count. They had a master toolroom where they kept all the new tools; they didn't count those every day. So I would steal whatever shovels, picks, hammers, and chisels I needed from the construction toolroom and have a buddy in the master toolroom replace them. When they inventoried that master toolroom, my buddy just changed the inventory count.

To recruit my tunnel diggers, I had to be sure I was getting real solid guys and no rats. Another buddy worked in the penitentiary record room, where they kept the files on 2,800 prisoners. When I'd get a guy in mind for the escape, I'd have this buddy check his record to be sure he wasn't a police informer. When I was sure he was clean, I'd approach him with the proposition. The ones I asked were all long-term prisoners and were agreeable to any plan that gave them even a fifty-fifty chance of escaping. That was the percentage I had put on my plan because mine wasn't the only tunnel in operation.

There was a standing joke there at the Atlanta penitentiary, "Don't jump up and down too hard, you might fall into someone's tunnel."

After we broke through the side of the manhole, we would take out the dirt in buckets and dump it in the sewer. As the water came from the washing machines in the laundry, the dirt was washed away with it. I could work fast and hard because I'd gotten into weightlifting. I went to the recreation yard every day and started wrestling and lifting weights to keep myself in shape. I won the heavyweight wrestling championship there in 1958.

The men would work for two hours; then another couple of guys would go down. I'd have to have clean clothes ready for them. That red clay would stick to them like wet paint. We were not very far from the walls when a friend told me he had a blueprint of all the steam tunnel and sewer lines.

"One of them goes to an outside warehouse, Frank! Perfect!"

"Forget it!" I told him. "All the tunnels that go outside the prison were blocked off long ago. These guys aren't stupid, you know. You have to think like us if you're going to be a guard here, don't you?" Matter of fact, that was one of the first things I'd checked out, those sewer and steam lines.

Well, this dumb ox didn't listen. One Saturday I was in the mess hall eating, and he came and whispered to me, "Another kid and I broke into the warehouse tunnel today, Frank!"

"Yeah? What happened."

"You know what happened. It was blocked up, like you said. The screw saw us. He thinks the other guy is you because you and me are together a lot."

"Thanks for tellin' me, pal. Yeah, thanks a lot."

Sunday a boy in my cell said a crowd of Cubans were giving him a hard time and he wanted to fight one of them.

"Hell, go ahead. I'll keep the rest of them off you."

I guess he knew I'd put a bunch of them in their place. There were plenty of Cubans in Atlanta—this was right when Castro was making such a big stink—and they ran in packs, all with razor blades and knives. One of them got put in the hole with me once and sat there spouting off about how sorry a place the United States was. I knew he was in prison for sneaking into this country.

"Listen, Pedro, or whatever damn fool name ya got, if you don't like the United States, you can take your black ass back out of it. Nobody bad-mouths America around me!"

He tied into me for that, and I knocked him out. He came to as they were hauling him to another cell.

"I get even with you, you bas'ard!"

"Next time I'll kill you!" I snapped at him. I'd already been in the hole for eleven days, and I was afraid they'd keep me there another eleven and I'd clean starve to death. In Atlanta they still didn't feed you when you were in the hole. Instead, the guard winked and said he hoped I'd kill the S.O.B. because he felt exactly the same way. I got out that afternoon.

But it wasn't over. One day in the showers, I saw the Cuban and his gang, looking as if they were laying for me. I walked right through the middle of them, and they didn't say a word or make a move.

So the boy and I went to the Cubans' cell, and he found the

one he wanted and hit him square in the mouth. I lined the others up against the wall. There was a hell of a lot of noise, and the guard came running, put the kid and the Cuban in the hole.

The word must have gotten around that I was a good guy to be on the right side of because another young fellow came around and asked me to go to court as a witness for him. He wanted me to say that he had bought his car from me instead of stealing it. It didn't matter to me. I had enough time piled up for a couple of decades—I might not even live that long. Two other men volunteered to be witnesses too. The three of us figured we could break out at the courtroom. And it would be a change of scene too.

The judge ordered us to appear in court in Tallahassee, Florida. We made quite a sight. Three carloads of Marshals, an F.B.I. car sniffing our tails, all three of us in leg-irons and cuffs. They put us in security cells in Tallahassee at the Federal prison there, a guard outside the door day and night. Makes a man feel mighty damn important. Next morning they handcuffed all three of us together, me in the middle.

"Just a precaution, Watson. If you run, you'll have to take your playmates with you."

"Fine. I enjoy their company. Yours too, officer."

At the courthouse, they'd blocked off both ends of the street. Federal Marshals, F.B.I. sleuths, two G.I.'s with tommy guns —quite a handsome reception. They put us in the Marshal's cells with a Marshal in front of the door with a sawed-off shotgun. News reporters clustered around like bees in a clover patch. All those flashbulbs made my eyes hurt.

"Frank Watson would bang these deputies' heads together and get out of here," the head Marshal told them. "That's why there's such tight security." I just grinned. It was true. I might have finished off a couple of the newsmen too.

The judge pounded for order. "All shotguns out of the courtroom, please! The officers may have pistols, but I will not have shotguns in my courtroom!"

I stuck to my testimony, but the other two guys were caught in a lie. The prosecuting attorney wanted to give all of us extra time for perjury, which made me laugh.

"I'm afraid we can't consider that, Mr. Prosecutor. Some of your witnesses were perjuring themselves too. But what I don't understand," the judge said with a big frown, "is how this trial ever got into my court in the first place. I have a letter from North Carolina that tells me that the witness Frank Watson is an outlaw, is considered extremely dangerous, and should not be taken out of prison for any reason whatsoever without a heavy guard. *Case dismissed!*"

Did he think we weren't under heavy guard? Hadn't he seen the parade?

They did us up in all that steel again—I never did see so much steel except in a solid wall—and took us back to Atlanta. It had been a very interesting trip. First time I was ever in Florida.

Later I found out that the boy we were lying for had put the finger on all of us for the F.B.I. That's what's known as Honor Among Thieves.

Ha Ha.

14

I PROBABLY KNEW IN MY GUT THAT I'D END UP AT ALCATRAZ sooner or later. It was a long train trip from Atlanta, first to Washington, D.C., then west in a Pullman with a half dozen Marshals. Five of us, three white and two black, cuffed hand and foot, chained to the rail of the bed at night. We had a terrific scheme worked out to escape from the train, but in the end it didn't work.

They did let us have reading matter. We took a staple from one of the books and picked the lock on one of the boys' cuffs. We planned to lock the door, hold a deputy against it, take the heavy water bottle and break the window so we could jump out. The train was going pretty slow because we were in the mountains around Lake Tahoe someplace. One of the colored boys, who always ate separately from us, ratted on us, and that did it.

Alcatraz, the Rock, has always been the end of the line. There had never been a successful escape across the choppy waters of San Francisco Bay with its dangerous currents, sharks, police, and boats. The word they used for the Rock was correct: *grim.*

I saw it first from the motor launch where we were under heavy guard. The weather was cold and foggy, with spooky sounds of horns through the mist, dark, big ships riding at anchor or coming into the Bay, the busy noise of the city fading away. All I could think of was *end of the line, end of the line.*

We docked at a small wharf, and they loaded us into a prison bus, our feet shackled so we took steps a couple inches long and jangled like a bunch of cows with bells on. The bus wound up a steep road, and we stopped at the main entrance of the cell block. At least we'd each have our own cell. Easier for them to watch us. Easier for the prisoners; we didn't have to try to get along with some of the crummy characters there. Easier to contain trouble.

We were allowed only the barest necessities. Everything else we owned was packaged until such time as we were released, which might well be never. Actually it may sound funny, but Alcatraz didn't really scare me any more than my present 102-pound wife does. It made me mad, and I looked on it as a challenge and by damn I'd meet it. I stood my ground behind those cruel walls for five years. They called me the Iron Man, among other things.

There was one large building, like a fort, with four cell blocks, a hospital, mess hall and kitchen, library, and offices for the prison staff. It held 260 men, the worst in the country, charged with every crime possible, some of them so terrible that they shouldn't be put in print. I thought that I was in my natural element with all those tough guys.

For the first year there I didn't work. I was kept locked up, allowed out to eat and take a shower. For a man like me, not working was the cruelest punishment of all. No recreation allowed either.

Behind the main cell block was a small yard with a high concrete wall. There were guard towers on two corners, an eight-foot chain-link fence around the top of the wall, and on top of that an accordion or roll of barbed wire. We played handball in that yard on weekends, or dominoes, checkers, chess. That was our recreation. When they began to let me work, the week consisted of jobs in the garment shop, glove

113

shop, brush shop, laundry, or machine shop. We were paid from twenty-four cents to a dollar an hour. Since we had no way of spending any money, we had to put it in a savings account, whether we wanted to or not. Some guys had been there long enough to feel as if they were rich in bank money.

The food was great. As good as any you could get in a San Francisco restaurant, they said. I'd never been in an S.F. restaurant, but I'm sure they were right. The food was served buffet style. After every prisoner had entered the mess hall and sat down at an eight-man table, they locked the door. Outside on a ten-foot catwalk was a guard with a .38 revolver and an automatic carbine. When we finished eating, officers counted the silverware. If one piece was missing, we had to sit until it was found. Going out, we'd have to walk through an electric eye to detect any metal on our bodies.

We wore wooden belt buckles. Our shoes were taken apart and all metal nails and steel arch supports were replaced by wood. Going to and from work we went through three electric eyes.

The only other good thing on the Rock beside the eats was the law library, one of the best in the United States. If a book we wanted wasn't there, we could send over to the library in San Francisco and get it. I didn't read much law, but I read everything else they let me get my hands on. Not much use working on the law. So far, it had always beat me. I had about fifty years piled up. I was still in my thirties, but fifty years would put me past eighty, even if no other time got added for prison troubles.

The hole at Alcatraz was something else. About nine by twelve, solid steel walls and floors, solid steel door. The toilet was a hole in the floor. The stench was horrible. No bed. At night you were given a mattress and a blanket, which were taken away in the morning. You could be in there any time from two weeks to a month, but some men had spent eighteen years or more in this well-designed little "treatment center." It was a perfect place to think and to hate. The Rock didn't supply you with the *Upper Room* and the Gideon Bible, so your mind couldn't go anyplace but into a pit of hell. Meals were half a head of cabbage and some water. You never saw any light unless a guard opened the door to see if you were still alive or to feed you your cabbage. Otherwise, pitch dark.

I was in the hole there three times. Conditions improved some during my five years. We finally got the same food as the mess hall. We didn't have any hot water and the bunks were solid steel, but they were better than the floor. One razor blade a week. If you lost it, you were put in the hole.

There was a good dental and medical program. Otherwise, the guys would have died like flies, and the government wouldn't have felt they had been really punished.

The guards with their families lived in apartments on the island. The prison launch ran to the mainland every hour, carrying children to school and back and taking any other person who wanted to go and wasn't locked up. Some of the men would break down and cry if they caught a glimpse of those kids with their school books and their bright wool caps. I never cried about anything. My own son was already in his teens. What was he like? Did he know his old man was one of the worst criminals in the U.S.A.? Did he care?

The first month I was there, two guys tried a break, guys that were almost trusties. They worked all over the island on the trash truck, with only one guard. They held knives against the guard's neck and tied him to a tree; then they tried to swim the S.F. Bay. The riptide is so strong there that I've seen it swallow up a 60-foot log.

One of them gave up and turned around to come back to the Rock, and of course the hole. The other drowned and wasn't found for a week. A Coast Guard cutter circled the island all the time he was missing. When they did locate him, he had washed up on shore in a little cave, and the crabs were eating him.

In 1959 they put me to washing pots and pans in the mess hall kitchen. At least I got all the pie and cake I could eat from a couple of the guys I knew in the bakery. Two of them came and told me they had tried to kill a colored boy in there.

"See, Frank, what we did was put a five-pound weight from the kitchen scales into a sock."

"Yeah, and we hit him a hell of a wallop, but the sock was rotten, and it tore—so the weight came out and knocked him cold. Cut his head wide open."

"We di'n't care. He'd already killed a coupla guys. So when he come to, him and two other blacks grabbed knives and come after us . . ."

"That's why we need a weapon, Frank. Anything!"

"How's about these three big potato mashers with inch-wide steel handles? They're three feet long. O.K.?"

We turned around, and there were the other guys coming at us. When they saw the potato mashers, they stopped cold. The guard came running, took the injured man to the hospital, the other two white men to the hole, and didn't pay any attention to me.

I learned a funny thing in Alcatraz about writing books. An old man who worked in the mess hall wrote one called *Rap Sheet* with stories about John Dillinger, Pretty Boy Floyd, Baby Face Nelson, and Ma Barker and her gang. It was really pretty well written; the only thing wrong was that the old fellow, who was in there for bank robbery, made himself one of the Dillinger gang. He wasn't at all. He'd gotten most of his stuff from "Creepy" Alvin Ray Karpis, one of the worst of the lot, whose cell was right above mine, and from Machinegun

Kelly, who'd served time there years before. It was true stuff, but the old gaffer hadn't been in on it. He should have stuck to facts.

You know how people love pets—dogs, cats, horses, birds. As a matter of fact, Robert Stroud, the Bird Man of Alcatraz, was there then. Some of the boys had mice and had them trained to do tricks at the snap of a finger. The mouse would turn a flip-flop or roll over and sit up like a dog. A young mouse would cost you three or four packs of cigarettes, but I never wanted one. Some prisoners need something to love, but no mouse for me.

One boy had a lizard with a silver chain around its neck. The mice had silver chains too. When the weather was nice, the boy would let his lizard out to sun itself. There are lots of seagulls around there, and one day one of them swooped down and ate the lizard, just like that. One gulp.

The boy, an Indian from Oklahoma in there for bank robbery, just sat there and cried. I felt so sorry for him. Some of the pet mice got eaten by seagulls too.

Killing pets wasn't the only things seagulls did. We'd be out in the recreation yard on weekends, and there'd be a couple hundred of them wheeling around and dropping shit on your head. When the guards found a gull's nest, they'd break the eggs. We hated the damn birds, but when we saw someone killing them, we were all for the gulls.

I played a lot of handball and did weightlifting to keep in shape, so I got the Captain to put me on the construction detail. After work, a lot of us weightlifters would work out in the laundry room. We talked the Captain into buying a 400-pound set of weights. He was a great guy, one of the best. He'd let me off every afternoon to lift weights and play handball, so I got pretty good at both of them. One day a Pro boxer came in as a prisoner, and they sent him to work in the laundry. He was cocky as hell, and I got tired of hearing him tell how great he was.

"I used to do a bit with the gloves myself," I told him. "Maybe I could learn a few tricks from you."

"Sure. Why not? Want to toss around a few punches?"

"Yeah. Why not?"

That guy had a worse temper than me. He got mad because he couldn't do anything with me, and he really slammed me over one eye and cut it open. That did it. I went over that cat like a truckload of bricks. I hit him in the mouth—twenty stitches it took—then I knocked him through a window and the glass cut his arm open—thirty stitches.

The Captain kept grabbing our arms and trying to break it up. He was covered with blood and hanging on to both of us. When we got cooled off and he broke us apart, the boxer told the doctor he'd fallen on the cement floor and cut himself. Captain said the same thing. What a man! I put a Band-Aid over my eye and told him I got hurt getting some wash out of the machine. All the guards grinned. They'd enjoyed the show. The boy was laid up for about two weeks; then we got to be friends because he was from the same part of Oklahoma that I was. Same stripe guy too.

The really big break at Ivy Bluff came that same year, 1959, and hit all the big news, but the police soon rounded them all up.

At the Rock they were bringing in more guys from Atlanta. I knew some of them. We started out trying to figure a way to beat the Rock. A rumor went around that you could act crazy and have yourself committed to the mental hospital at Springfield, Missouri, where it was easy to escape. Some of them already had mental records, but not me. They tried. They learned a lesson. It didn't work.

The nut doctor went over me with his little hammers and his dumb questions, then just laughed when the officer asked him about me.

"There's nothing wrong with this man," he said, blinking through his eyeglasses. "Sane as you and me, I'd guess. Which means, I think you are doing the right thing by keeping an eye on him."

"Thanks, Doc. Glad to see you appreciate me."

"I wouldn't think of doing anything else, Watson. You are a man who bears being appreciated."

I never did know what he meant.

Everyone got two packs of Wings cigarettes a week. I didn't smoke, so I always gave mine away. Men were sometimes killed in fights over cigarettes. Speaking of that, there was a girlboy and his daddy both in there, working in the machine shop. They were screwing each other, but they both had such short peckers that they invented a pecker-stretcher. It was run on fifty pounds of air pressure with an air gauge that had a red warning signal if it went past the fifty pounds.

I happened to catch them using it one day. It could take a five- or six-inch dick and stretch it to a foot. One time the red signal popped up and I got the hell out of there. The thing might explode and cover us all with pecker.

I never did get mine stretched. My women always thought mine was just about right. The fee for the job was two packs of Wings cigarettes for every inch of dick.

After a couple of years, they began sprucing up the place. We got beds with springs, got our cells painted and new toilets and sinks. Hot water in every cell, too. We prisoners were doing all the painting and everything, so some of us set up some escape plans.

Part of the job was putting in new toilets and sinks, and

adding hot water meant putting in new pipes. We used an electric jackhammer to drill bigger holes in the walls of the cells that were to get new equipment. The foreman was supposed to watch us every minute, but he didn't. When he was called to another cell, we jackhammered a hole big enough for a man to crawl through in any cell where the man was planning to escape. Then we filled the hole with toilet paper or whatever we could find and covered it with a thin coat of plaster. As soon as the plaster was dry, we'd paint over it and remove any signs of hanky-panky.

I knew I was too big to get through the ventilator at the shaft top. I helped finish the job anyway, but it about broke my heart to decide to give up. Maybe somebody up there did like me—I believe that every man who made it to the water that night died in that treacherous Bay. They must have.

The morning after the escape, every man in the prison was waiting with anticipation for the alarm to go off. They all knew it, but not one man informed the authorities.

We had made dummy heads with wet paper fashioned into the shape of human heads and allowed them to dry and then added a couple of touches of paint that might look like faces in the gloom of a cell. For sanitary reasons they had cut all our hair in the barber shop, so we took that hair and glued it to the dummies.

The guys broke up through the hole and got on to the roof with ropes. One of them was late, so the other three got scared the guard would see them and went down, taking the ropes with them. The poor kid was stuck up there, three stories high, in the freezing cold, all night.

The guards didn't miss anyone until the head count the next morning. When one of the men didn't answer, the guard reached into the cell to shake him awake and got hold of that dummy head. All hell broke loose. Worst uproar they ever had.

The Coast Guard circled the island, and the Army shook down everything and everyone. All they ever found was the poor shivering kid on the roof and three homemade life jackets floating in the water. The wind had been very high that night, and the waves were fierce.

When the escape was found out, even though it failed, the prisoners clapped hands and shouted. They knew the guards would be furious.

As I said earlier, no one ever escaped from the Rock.

Several days later, the F.B.I. showed up and questioned several known escape artists, including me.

"What about it, Watson?"

"Listen, if I'd known about any escape, I'd sure enough have been with them."

"Frank, you couldn't even get your head through that hole those guys went through. They all had to be skinny to make it."

He was right. Both of us knew it.

In the forties, fifties, and maybe the early sixties, one of the ways the North Carolina prisoners got attention was to cut their heel strings to protest prison conditions. They asked me to do that at Alcatraz, but I turned them down.

"Not on your life," I told them. "I like to escape too much for that. I need heel strings to help run. I might cut somebody else, but I'll never cut myself."

15

W‍E'D BEEN HEARING RUMORS THAT THEY WERE GOING TO CLOSE up the Rock because everything was falling apart. The sea air rusted out whatever they had just painted, and there was never enough money to do all the necessary repairs. One day the foreman called me over and said I was on a chain. A chain is a transfer.

"On a chain? You're full of shit. They're not going to transfer me out of this Garden of Eden."

"Oh, yes they are. You and nine others. Next Monday. Better go pack your undies."

"Monday? I'm getting moved Monday? *Next week?*"

"Right!"

"Where to?"

"Atlanta. Your old home base."

But it wasn't right, because on Monday they began having all that trouble at the University of Mississippi. The Border Patrol plane they were going to use to fly us out had to be used to take the U.S. Marshals down to Jackson, Mississippi. I sat on the Rock another two weeks, sizzling mad, and that foreman got suspended for two weeks for telling us we were going.

They finally came for us about four in the morning, handcuffed us, put us on the prison launch, took us across that brutal stretch of water that had claimed so many men, set us on the dock, and herded us to the bus that would take us to the airport. Guards, U.S. Marshals, the usual bristling escort, lined up along the way. Didn't want to lose any of this precious cargo, or Uncle Sam would be mad.

The plane was an old World War II DC-3. It still flew. Ah, those friendly skies! They had a Border Patrol crew, pilot and copilot, five guards, a doctor, and ten of us. Everyone was airsick as we bumped along, so the doc gave us some pills. I probably haven't taken twenty pills in my whole life—I hate medicine or any kind of drug—but those helped. We stayed all night at Leavenworth at the elegant hotel the government keeps there for its bad boys. I saw some of my old buddies in the mess hall.

Next day we flew to Atlanta, a very happy bunch. At least I was off the Rock, the only way I could get off. At Atlanta, they were all scared to death of us. You'd have thought we were a bunch of wild tigers escaped from their cage.

After they'd checked me out, they sent me before the prison classification board to see what kind of work I should do.

"Well, Watson, you going to try to get along a little better here?" the deputy warden asked me. "I see by your record that you don't do too well anyplace. Alcatraz said dangerous."

"If you let me alone, I'll let you alone," I said.

"You're too big for anyone to bother you too much. Somebody said your friend, gangster Mickey Cohen, helped you get a coat big enough for you at the Rock."

"Yeah. He worked in the clothing room. Saw that I had big sweat shirts too. Not many clothes come in size 52. Nice guy, Mickey."

"So I hear. How about the cotton mill? Would you like to work there?"

"Not much. I might like the canvas shop, making mailbags."

"O.K. We'll start you in the steel room, cutting steel for the mail carts. I understand you're an artist at cutting steel. No use wasting such a specialized talent."

It was a first-class job, as prison jobs go. And I kept on with my weightlifting and handball. I got several offers to escape, but I kept saying I'd think it over. Maybe getting off the Rock and into a halfway decent kind of work changed me a little. Not much, but a little.

Christmas 1962—I was 41—I sent a Christmas card to my first wife and my son Johnny. Not many days later the guard called me and said I had a visitor.

"You're kiddin'! I ain't had a visitor in years. Are you sure it's for me?"

"Of course I'm sure! Would I lie to you?"

"Yes."

"It's your wife. Git on out there before she leaves."

I thought it would be Angie. I'd forgotten about the card. I hadn't seen Betty Sue in ten years, and Angie had always been good about visiting me.

"It's me, Frank. Don't you know me? It's Betty Sue. And this is Johnny, your son Johnny!"

Well, when you're not expecting *anyone*, and then you're expecting a wife, and it turns out to be a different wife—well—

"Johnny has always wanted to see his daddy, and when that card come—" Her eyes were full of tears. I looked up at this tall, handsome, *decent* kid and I couldn't say anything.

Finally I said, "Hello, Johnny."

"H'lo, Dad."

"You sure look fine, Son."

"You look pretty good, Dad. Mom said you would."

I couldn't face the boy any more, so I asked Betty Sue if she'd remarried.

"No, Frank. I'm a one-man woman. When I got married, it was for life. But even if I was married to someone else, I'd come to see you. You need someone to visit you, Frank. I've prayed for you a lot."

124

"*Prayed* for me?"

"And I've taught Johnny to respect you and love you. Well, when I compare you with any other man I ever met, I—"

"How do I come out, Betty Sue?" I asked, half-laughing and at the same time knowing what she'd probably say.

"At the top. Every time."

When they left, I walked back to my cell and flopped down on my bed with my face to the wall, tears in my eyes.

She'd written the warden to ask if she could come, and he had told her yes, any time she wanted to, and to be sure to bring the boy, already seventeen years old. So she'd come. And said she'd come again. That warden was an O.K. guy.

But then—well, Angie got word I was in Atlanta, and *she* wrote the warden to ask if she could come see me, and he said yes, of course, it would be good for Frank. And being Angie, she came.

Women!

I don't blame the warden. He was doing his best, but both these women got mad about the other one coming to see me, and after all, I wasn't married to either of them. They'd both divorced me because I was a jailbird; now all of a sudden they both wanted me.

You may think that's a great state to be in. It isn't. All three of those people, two women and a wonderful son, were all working on me to get me to go to church. *Church!* The place would cave in or go up in smoke if old sinner Frank Watson hung around there.

They'd start quoting scripture to me. Kind of set them all back when I could quote a damn sight more of it than they could, and get it straight too. My God, hadn't that been my only reading matter for days and weeks and months? Hadn't it been the one thing that kept me from going off my rocker down there in those holes? If the Devil could quote scripture, so could Frank Watson, by the hour.

I went to church, there in the prison. It was easier than thinking up excuses and having those three at me all the time. I hated the chaplain. His name was Tucker, but we called him Cedar Arm because he had only one arm. I guess I hated Cedar Arm Tucker because he was so damn human and because he told it like it was, reason enough not to trust him.

He'd come to visit, kick around a few words, talk about anything big or little, bring books he thought I'd like, things like *Don Camillo* or books about the astronauts, General Patton, John Kennedy, or Western forts. He knew I hated everyone, but he was the first one to understand that I really hated myself. I was a rotten guy. He was the first person I met in all those years of prison who saw anything in me but violence and hatred.

If anyone knew the uselessness of punishment and the need for some kind of hope, even tiny sparks of hope, it was Cedar Arm. I grew to respect that man as I have never respected any man in my life. I never got around to telling him because I was paroled back to North Carolina, but I got so I would go into that chapel, a prison chapel not at all beautiful, and sit, just sit. I could find peace. Peace. I didn't know how much I needed it.

One day I was in the mess hall and looked up to see Mickey Cohen! He came and shook hands with me. He was a great guy, a nice person—I mean nice as people like us go. People outside in the free world may not realize it, but there are some fine people in prison. I've met a few I'd trust my life to. Some crumbs, too. All kinds in there, like everywhere. Yeah, I know some real toughs who don't want the prison people to know anything. If they can't handle it themselves, they sure don't want the cops to be in on it. I guess I'm that kind.

One of the boys in my cell thought he was a plenty tough cat. I had to beat that out of him. He had a buddy who wanted to back him up and help him, so I knocked him out too and sat and read the paper until he came to, and then I knocked him out again. He soon got the idea. It just takes a little longer for some.

Robert F. Kennedy came to the prison while I was in Atlanta. He was so easy to talk to. Several of us told him we'd been working to get ourselves paroled back to North Carolina. The chaplain had been talking to people and writing letters here and there, and the warden had been helping, but no luck. None of us realized how much Cedar Arm Tucker had been doing for us behind the scenes. He was never a guy to show his hand on that stuff.

"Write to me at my office in Washington," RFK told us, "and we'll check into it." He did.

The prisons were always asking for more money to build more facilities to lock up more people. "You've got parole boards," President Kennedy told them. "Try using them." And Robert Kennedy said the same thing. Those two men did more for prisoners than any President and Attorney General in history.

When both of them were murdered, I felt pretty bad. Some of the punks in prison went around laughing when JFK was killed. I told them to stay out of my way or there'd be some broken jaws. Crumbs like that don't have any pride or class. They've never learned to blame themselves for their troubles.

A lot of the Mafia big shots were in Atlanta. I got to know a few of them, and that was enough. I learned one thing: never get involved with the Mafia. You can't win. No way.

North Carolina didn't particularly want us back, but they had to take me when the Federal Parole Board said to take me or free me. It had taken eight years. A doctor in training would have finished med school in that time.

I thought a lot about my son. Could I ever see him again?

How was he doing? Had he been too disappointed in seeing me? I could hardly believe that such a wonderful kid was mine. I sure hadn't done much for him.

When I got back to Raleigh and Central Prison on August 25, 1964, it was like coming home in a way, but nobody seemed very glad to see me. Well, I was used to that. They kept me locked up for three months, not even letting me out on the yard.

I had to get something to do, so one day I just walked off and went to see Major O'Neal in his office.

"How'd you get here?"

"I was carrying out trash and here I am."

"If you don't get out of this office at once, I'll put you on death row with some of the tough boys we've got there." At this time death row was also the lockup.

I didn't move, just stood there politely. "If you want to lock me up, Major, go ahead. I'm used to it. But I need to work, to get some useful job in prison. I'm wasting my whole damn —my whole life sitting here."

He kind of hesitated. "Well, go back to your cell before you get into any more trouble, and I'll think about it."

That night I got my job badge and an assignment to work in the print shop. I felt as if I might be on my way. I didn't know where to, but I was moving.

16

AT CENTRAL PRISON, I STARTED GOING TO CHURCH EVERY SUNDAY! I couldn't believe it myself. And they sent me to cooking school to give me another way of earning my living if I ever got out. It also gave me a pretty decent job behind walls. I'm a damn good cook, if you like things in quantity.

In 1965 I tried to get a new trial, but it was denied. Having been an Outlaw and on the Ten Most Wanted List isn't a gilt-edged recommendation for much of anything. Pitt Sluder, the police chief in Asheville, had told Angie that he'd see to it that I was never free as long as I lived and she'd better get herself another man.

"I'll tell you this, both of you," I yelled at them. "I'll live to piss on all your graves, you bastards!"

In spite of all that bad-mouthing from Sluder, the new police chief there had actually come to see me when they brought me back to Asheville from Wyoming after I was captured. Brought me candy and books and never once asked what I had done, the only guy that paid any attention to me at all. Funny how I hated him and all his kind, and I suppose he hated me, yet he was that decent to me. Never could figure it out.

He and the U.S. Marshal both told me that if I got free it would be darned smart for me to move someplace else, far away. I'd plumb worn out North Carolina. At the same time, their records on me were what kept me from getting a new trial.

In the time I'd been gone, conditions in the lockup had changed. I guess you might say improved. At least they were different. I think that lady judge had a lot to do with it. They had finally started feeding the men on their Punitive Segregation, the hole. They called it Monotonous Diet, so it would still be punishment but not such downright cruelty, they told themselves.

Here's the way they did it: ground-up liver, onions, carrots, turnips, and God knows what else, maybe a rat or two because they had plenty, all mixed together, cooked into the most ungodly mess you can imagine. You could smell it coming and it would make you puke. Then they'd get after you for not eating it. I'd rather starve, no fooling.

Maybe what changed their minds was the system of *muling* (from the word *mule*). At Central Prison, the segregation cell block, the hole, backs up to the cell block for the general prison population. Between them is a corridor for sewer and water pipes. The toilets in the hole were connected to the other cells by the sewer line.

Suppose I was on segregation. A man in the main cell block whose cell was back to back with mine would take all the water out of his toilet with the tin cup they gave him, and I'd take all the water out of mine the same way. We could then talk to each other through the toilets.

"How many men in there now?" he'd ask.

"Four."

"What kind of cigarettes, candy, food do they want? Have you got a list?"

"Yeah. Ready?"

Then I'd tell him, so many packs of Chesterfields or Camels or whatever he could get, eight candy bars, any food he could find that was wrapped up, and so forth.

Then we'd transport the stuff by a mule, which is a long cord, or strips of blankets or sheets tied together so it can reach from one end of the cell block to the other. It is rolled into a ball and can be unrolled to the other end. The man in the far cell catching it can reel it in.

It takes two mules to make the system work. I'd flush mine down the toilet, and the guy with the food would do the same. When the two mules came together in the sewer line, they'd get entangled, and I could then pull in my mule with his fastened to it. We might have to do it several times before they got hooked together tight enough.

Once hooked up and sure that his mule was in my cell, he'd tie empty Bull Durham sacks at about one-foot intervals, then fill them with candy, boiled eggs, cigarettes. At his signal I'd pull it into my cell. It might take all night.

The screws knew about it, of course, and were always trying to catch us. We'd get a man who was celling near the door of the cell block to warn us by whistling or singing.

After muling all night, I'd divvy up whatever I had among all the men in segregation. If you were caught, you could get an extra thirty days in the hole, and the man who muled the things to you from the main cells was liable to get thirty days in segregation himself. We did it anyway. We had to live.

After the loot was distributed, I'd spend the day sleeping and eating my share of the night's haul. "I was in prison and ye fed me," I'd read someplace in the Bible. Grandpa Cook would have cackled to know I was fed by a system of muling.

Along in 1966 I got out of the print shop and into Recreation, in charge of all the athletic equipment. The boss was a damn good guy, and he'd back me up in anything as long as I was right. By this time, I was top bull. I ran all the rackets: gambling, numbers, loan business, bootlegging. I had part of the leather goods business—ladies' purses, and so forth. The guards ran the outer perimeter with guns. I ran the inner perimeter of the prison population.

The next year I asked to be sent to a road camp. I was tired of looking at the same gray walls, and I'd be a little closer to where I considered home, Asheville. I had years and years yet to serve, but I'd been proving I could stay out of trouble if I wanted to. Funny, I wished I had a picture of my son, just a picture.

Of course there were times I had trouble, and my temper was still at a low boiling point, so I'd slug some cat now and then when guys would make me blow my stack.

It was eleven years since I'd been in Burnsville Prison Camp. They were building new roads, cutting heavy timber, and clearing brush. It was a month before I was back in shape, in spite of all the weightlifting and boxing at Central. They worked the living hell out of us at Burnsville. Every day one or two men would land in the hole for not working hard enough. I loved those mountains. Just being there was enough for me at that point. There was even a small touch of peace now and then.

One day when I was working on the main highway, a little sports car streaked by, slammed on its brakes, and skidded to a stop. It was Angie's boy!

"Frank! How long ya been here?"

"Three, four months I guess."

"Why didn't you let Mom know?"

"Oh, I guess I didn't want to bother her. I've made enough trouble for her and everyone else."

"That's not true, Frank. We'll come to see you Sunday!"

It was great. After all, Angie is some kind of woman, and she was downright glad to see me. My stepson's wife and tiny baby were there. They let me hold him.

"I'm scared I'll break him! I never get to hold anything this little, and wiggling at that. You'd better take him back. I'm used to picks and shovels and rock hammers, not babies!" They all laughed.

Burnsville was still a hard place. Eight or ten of the guys

thought they were real stags, white panther and black panther types, the kind that can't get along anywhere. They kept pushing until I knew the only way to settle it was to go straight for their asses.

There was this cat just back from Viet Nam in the Marines, and he kept cutting off the hot water while I was showering so he could brush his teeth with the cold water. I finally right-hooked him in the mouth, and we went at it. I hit him with a right, then a left, and dazed him; then I followed with an overhand right. You've seen those big trash cans? The last time I hit him, he went headfirst into one of those.

One of his buddies charged me from behind, so I turned, hit him a hard right, and he ran back to the end of the cell block. I checked to make sure he stayed there, and by that time the first guy was crawling out of the trash can. I caught him in the ribs with a left hook and crossed a right to his jaw. Back into the trash can! I waited until he got out again, then I really laid into him.

"*Frank!* Don't hit him any more! Frank! You'll kill him!" It was an honor-grade buddy in the next cell block.

I didn't say anything, just kept belting him with right- and left-hand punches.

"You want to lose all the good time you've got piled up?" My buddy's voice finally got through to me. I cooled off as quick as I got mad. The guy was in terrible shape. Blood was coming out of his ears and nose, and he had two or three broken ribs. He was in the sick room nearly two weeks.

He was twenty years old and weighed a little over two hundred pounds. I was forty-five and weighed the same. The old Cherokee temper was going to finish me yet. And probably someone else. One of the other guys asked me if it wasn't maybe an *Apache* temper. He grew up in the West. The Apaches are worse than the Cherokees.

When I got control of myself, I looked down at my hands.

One of the knuckles on my right hand was driven back into my wrist. I could hardly use that hand for months.

Angie and her family came to see me every weekend. She always let me know she'd take me back, but I told her she'd had me once and that was enough. She married another guy after she divorced me, but then she divorced him too, maybe hoping I'd change my mind.

Whipping the shit out of one stag didn't do it. They got so bad that I had to straighten one out almost every night. I right-handed one of them in the nose, and the blood flew all over me. He ran to the front of the cell block and told the guard I broke his nose, with me right on his tail. He turned and threw a punch, but I kept going in on him. We finally stopped fighting after I got through whipping hell out of him. The guard looked him over and said his nose wasn't broken, but the Captain called me on the carpet.

"What's the trouble, Watson?"

"No trouble at all, Cap'n."

"You're in at least one fight a day, every day, Watson. Bad ones. The only way you can talk is with your fists. It's gotta stop. I'm gettin' plenty of beefs from Raleigh about you."

"The fightin' can stop any time, Cap'n, soon as these stags find out they ain't kings around here."

"That ain't quite it, Watson. You're the type guy that just has to fight, but how about fightin' a little easier so I don't have to get rid of you?"

"Get rid of me? You ain't got many more places to send me!"

Billy was a black boy. He and his gang had been bad-mouthing whites until I called their bluff with a knife and a few special words, but four or five months later he came around to ask me if I'd help him. I said sure, why not?

"You see, Frank, I got five years yet."

"So what? I got plenty myself. Five years ain't nothin'!"

"I want to get a buddy of mine to cut off my foot while we're out on the road."

"Why'n hell do you want to do somethin' stupid like *that*? You can't be much more'n eighteen or nineteen years old."

"You get six months off your sentence for every toe and finger you lose. Didn't you know that?"

"Well, I'll be damned."

"Will ya do it, Frank? You're the fork man. When the guards aren't looking at me but watching you pulling the trees and brush across the road, let me know."

"You that crazy to get out, Billy? Are you damn sure?"

"Damn sure."

"O.K. If that's what you want."

The foreman went somewhere in the truck and the guard was talking to the water boy, so I gave the signal. The boy cutting brush right beside Billy went *whack!* with his bush axe. He cut off half the boy's foot. A five-year sentence canceled. I can still hear it.

Seems as if I was right back in my old habits, telling off the new foreman, helping guys escape but not getting caught, and never figuring out the right way to get myself out. Finally, I said the hell with it. Then they ran me in for disobeying a direct order and shipped me off to Craggy Prison Camp at Asheville to stay in the hole for twenty-five days.

While I was there, Central Prison in Raleigh blew wide open with a riot that killed six men, wounded seventy or eighty, damaged the prison chapel, and stirred up holy hell. Most of us knew it was coming. I'm glad I wasn't there, because I'd have been right in the midst of it and probably got my ass shot off.

At Craggy I went into a new business. I stole a thirty-cup coffee pot so I could sell coffee and sandwiches to a long-running poker game I'd gotten started. The same old trouble started. I split a guy's lip when he told me to go to hell. He'd been losing in the poker game.

"I'd be glad to, you son of a bitch, but I can't stand your mother's cooking," I told him. So he tied into me again, and I laid him flat. That time they moved me to North Wilkesboro. I wanted to stay at Craggy—I didn't have any worse trouble there than anywhere else—so I could see Angie and her family, but you don't get your wants in this game.

17

AFTER I WAS AT NORTH WILKESBORO FOR A WHILE, I ACTUALLY got to liking it. It was the best camp I'd ever been in. I was in a good work squad, my foreman had been a preacher, the guard was a good man. I've never let any of my people send me money, so I had to hustle for it. The gambling-coffee-sandwich business was the best thing I'd hit.

By 1969 I was making good money with a poker game going every night and extra business on the weekend. As usual a guy came around and wanted to know if I'd like to escape.

"I dunno," I said. "I'm pushin' for honor-grade and I got about five hundred bucks in my stash. I better sit tight."

"You must not have heard the news, Frank."

"News? They turnin' us loose?"

"Hell, no! They *like* us!"

"Bringin' in a freightload of broads?"

"Yeah, they are. But first they're gonna transfer all gun-grade prisoners, you real toughies, over to Asheboro Prison Unit."

"Is that straight?"

"Pre-zactly. Next month."

"O.K. First we'll figure out some rides. I've got a billfold made with a secret compartment so I can keep my five hundred. The lousy five bucks they let us draw a week wouldn't get us very damn far."

Well, I lined up three rides, and every one of them failed. I got into a string of fights and gave a couple of guys split lips, broke another one's arm, and really tore into one cat who would peek into the window of the cell block on visiting days. He was always trying to look up under the women's dresses and making dirty comments out loud. I love to look at the ladies, you know, but talk like that doesn't set well with me. The ladies are what makes life worth while for the men, right? Right!

I laid him flat. I thought I'd killed him. The guard got a couple of guys to lift him onto a bed, and we all watched until he started twitching his fingers and groaning. That ended the peeking. He was lucky he could ever open his eyes again.

It took a long time, but we didn't give up and finally we got away. We caught the guard on a sharp curve where he couldn't see part of the work squad, and off we went. They brought the dogs and ran us until our tongues hung out. It was sundown before they caught us, on the other side of the mountain. They shook us down, but they didn't find my money.

Like always, the Captain called me in. "Why'd ya run this time, Frank? Ya bin doin' right well."

"I needed a little vacation, Cap'n. The scenery around here is so purty, but I ain't seen near all of it I'd like to—"

"Guess I don't blame you," he said with a big sigh. "I'd like to see somethin' diffurnt m'self. Well, they've got a nice comfy place for you in Raleigh. It's called G Block. Nice change from these open spaces."

Four months on G Block, then the Central Classification Committee, the CCC. They decided they'd try me out at Caledonia Prison Farm, northeast of Raleigh, close to the Virginia line. I'd never been there. I worked at farm labor for about a week; then they put me in the laundry. I began working out on the weights again, getting myself in shape. Three of my buddies from other camps were there, so we started making the usual plans to break out. One of them had two homemade .22 pistols, single shot.

"We'll complain about a toothache," I decided. "They'll have to take us into Roanoke Rapids to the dentist. Then we'll throw down on the guards, take the van, and leave. I've got this ground-down file too, sharp as a razor."

"We're with ya!"

"I think it sounds pretty good," I admitted.

A couple of them thought we ought to do it a different way. An honor-grader had a real .38 brought in by his girl friend. I went to him and asked him how much he wanted for it. I had quite a bankroll by then.

"I sent it back," he told me. "She took it home with her."

"How much would it take to get her to bring it again?"

"Maybe a hundred bucks."

"It's a deal."

He told her, but she decided her dear boy might get hurt and she wouldn't get it for me. Why did she give it to him in the first place? When you've got a gun, it isn't for stirrin' mint juleps. So that took care of that.

Once I actually helped a guard settle a bunch of drunks. He couldn't handle it, so I yelled out, called 'em a few special flattering names, gave 'em a few threats, and it was over. Next day the Major called me in, after he'd put the worst drunks in the hole. The Major was a pretty good cat, even if he was a prison official. If he said something, it was right.

"Frank, seems to me that every time there's trouble, your name seems to come into it. I'm not blaming you—you've got a lot of power—but I know, and you know, that if you gave the word, the prisoners would tear this place down."

"Right, Major. It'd take maybe ten minutes. But I don't want to see any of my buddies hurt."

"Well, how about staying here instead of putting in for that transfer you asked for a month or so ago?"

"I got folks up near Craggy, Major. I can have visits."

Maybe this didn't have anything to do with the story, but

maybe it did, because right after that, Christmas, 1970, a buddy's mother and sister came to see him and brought Christmas dinner. They asked me to eat with them. A real family meal! When they were ready to leave, the mother hugged my neck, and then the girl hugged my neck. She was a real fine little girl, pretty as a picture. They lived in Raleigh. I thought for a while there might be some of those sparks of light I'd been looking for ever since I used to try to sing in Cedar Arm Tucker's choir in Atlanta. To be part of a family, even if it wasn't my family, for just that meal was—

They let me go to Craggy, but in a week they called me to Central Prison to meet with the CCC and sent me to Monroe Prison Camp in Union County at the edge of the mountains.

The situation there was plenty hot. Ninety-five blacks and fifteen or twenty whites, the whole place flaming with hate. I was there a month or so before the real fight got going. I stopped the first one, between a white and a black, and the guard put them both in the hole; then about ten or twelve blacks jumped me. At first they thought I had a knife. I wished I had!

Six of them picked up a locker that must have weighed two hundred pounds and threw it at me. I threw it right back. Then about twenty more showed up. I couldn't handle that big a crowd, so I got hell beat out of me. The guards got so scared they ran outside. Only a buddy named Tommy stuck by me.

After they got the place calmed down and had me sewed up, I decided that it was a pretty yellow bunch of white men when only one of them had guts enough to help me.

I got a new angle to my hatred. I had to keep fighting myself every minute so I wouldn't beat hell out of every black I saw. We didn't use to have race problems in prison. Mixing them up mixed us all up—it's bad, very bad. A couple of blacks who were good friends of mine came and apologized for the ones who had jumped me. As for the rest of them, there wasn't a real man in the bunch or they'd have fought me single-handed. Maybe they knew who'd win.

They had to take Tommy and me to Raleigh to the hospital. My head was swollen so bad I couldn't see. All I could think of was to get back to Monroe Prison Camp and finish the job.

I'd lie in the hospital bed figuring. I had to take care of every bastard out there. First, I'd escape to the camp at night, lock up the guards, get out the few friends I had there, white and black, and kill all the rest with hand grenades, shotguns, or anything I could lay my hands on. After finishing that, I'd find their families and get rid of them too.

When I got out of the hospital, they put me on H Block in the West Wing at Central, the worst place there. Every waking moment I talked to myself like this: *Do they call this re-habilitating prisoners? Whatever the N.C. Prison System has anything to do with turns to shit. And that goes for every damn official from Commissioner Lee Bounds right down the list to every dirty bastard who has his stinkin' ass anyplace in the whole fuckin' system.*

After your mind has wallowed around in that kind of crap for twenty-four hours a day, there isn't much to work with.

That must have been when I finally hit bottom, the lowest pit I could get into. I thought I'd hit bottom a hundred times, but nothing was ever like that. Hate was eating me up; my guts were crowded full of it. I knew then what *hell* was. I thought I already knew, but those other hells had only been purgatories on the way there.

I got paper and pencil and did a little arithmetic. I put down every day of time I'd served since that first sentence in my teens. The time I was out and on the run didn't count, just

141

what I'd spent in prison. The figure got bigger and bigger, and finally I added it up—over twenty-seven years. I was crowding fifty.

What had I done that amounted to anything I could be proud of? My son, yes. But I'd only provided the start for him, not done one thing further for him. Except maybe stay out of his sight. I had gotten myself called every kind of scum, criminal, outlaw—that should be in capital letters the way the Law does it: *Outlaw*—rotter, low-down skunk, sneak-thief, rattlesnake. I was an "artist." At what? Escaping. Scheming. Cheating. Lying. *Fighting.*

Still bandaged from the last knock-down-drag-out, I lay on my cell bed and started to pray. I'd prayed before, maybe a thousand times, but I had never meant it. I had tried to mean it, but I didn't seem to know how. I wanted to pray for real help for all my troubles, but none ever seemed to come, or if it did, I didn't recognize it or wouldn't accept it. Maybe I was afraid to. Taking help might make me look weak, or something less than a man. I don't know.

That night I put my hands over my face and said, "Lord, *help me! Help* me! *Forgive* me!" My eyes and face burned with the agony of my prayer. "*Help me!! I can't go on alone! I need someone, Lord!*"

This part is hard to tell, but I've been honest about everything else, so I'll be honest about this. Whether you believe it or not doesn't matter. All I know is that it happened.

I don't know how long I prayed this same desperate prayer: help-me-help-me-I-can't-go-on-*help*-me! After a while I opened my eyes to the gray walls, and there above me, on the ceiling, was a face. Just a face, full of understanding and gentleness—well, I can't describe that either. There wasn't any sound or any voice like Saul heard in the Bible, no thunder and lightning, just quiet. *Quiet.*

I looked at that face for maybe a minute; then I turned over and went to sleep, full of peace. Or did I dream it? I couldn't have.

The next day people around me seemed easier to live with. Perhaps it was because I was easier to live with. I began to admit, deep down inside me, that all those names they called me, any name they called me, *all* of them, had been right. Alcatraz had put "Homicidal" on my record. Well, I was, wasn't I? Murderous? And not just on the Rock.

I had no idea what might happen next. For all those first fifty years of my life I hadn't given a hootin' damn. I figured my life was ruined anyway. Now I had the strange feeling of being actually excited about what might come next. The peace that had helped me was still there. My life wasn't over. Only the bad part.

18

SOMETHING, I'LL NEVER BE QUITE SURE WHAT, STARTED ME UP out of that dark cave I was floundering in. On H Block they started some discussion groups, supervised by staff people from the mental health division of the prison. It was a good place to gripe and blow off steam. Cuss out the world and everyone in it! You could come out loud and strong against anything and everything you hated: the prison administration, Mr. Bounds, law-and-order, squares, rats, females.

I went just to get out of my cell before I went clear nuts. I probably was the loudest yeller they had because I really sounded off, but then everyone did. I have a powerful pair of lungs and I used 'em. After a while we got to talking about ourselves and each other, what was wrong with us, why we were like we were. Man, that was poisonous. It was like being skinned alive. I found out that a lot of guys felt the same thing about themselves that I did about myself, *hatred.*

The group gradually changed from a bitch session into sensible talk about the prison system, what could be done to get some of us no-goods straightened out. I couldn't see it at the time because I was so blindly despising everything, but somehow I was starting uphill.

"Frank, you don't have to go around trying to kill everyone just so you can be king!"

"I don't kill people, you bastards!"

"You try to. And you damn near do. It's only luck—"

"King? I don't want to be no *king!*"

"Hell, whaddaya call it? Emperor?"

"*No!* I just like to have things around me in good order!"

"You're a goddam bully, that's all!"

I started after them; then they all began to laugh. Nobody likes to be laughed at. It was damn hard to take.

During that time we had five or six bad fights on H Block, so we'd talk about them at these bull sessions. We began to see that we fought because of all the frustration and bitterness and hopelessness. We were really hitting out at all those gray walls and a thousand other things we couldn't get away from.

Two of the guys got into it bad in the mess hall. One of the guards was fixing to shoot tear gas, and the second was ready to use his club. Two of us started talking to the guys, and they quieted down. Kind of funny to see it work! It was easy!

Of course, it was back to the Captain's office. I about fell out when he said, "Nice work, Watson!"

"What work?"

"Stopping the fight in the mess hall. It would have been a humdinger if you hadn't. We don't like to use the gas, you know, but after that riot in '68 we're all like some gun-shocked old dog. As soon as he hears a sound, he wants to bite something."

"It was nothing, sir. Glad to do it," I said, feeling silly because I had called a Captain "sir." I must be slipping.

"Mr. Bounds and I have decided that you and your buddy are to have ninety days' good time off your sentences."

"*Shit!*" I blurted out before I thought how it sounded. "Sorry, sir, I meant to say thank you. I've never had any extra good time off for anything in all these twenty-five years in prison."

"Right. I understand."

Thirteen months on H Block; then I went before the CCC again for assignment.

"Well, Watson, where do you want to work?"

"In the kitchen, if that's O.K. I've been to cook school."

"Fine. We'll put you on Number Three gain time. That would mean that your remaining time would be cut in just about half."

"*What?*"

"Number Three gain time."

"I could be free in a couple of years? I haven't been that close in eighteen years!" I thought I'd better watch my language, so I said, "Wow!"

"We might put you on the second shift so you can have more time for your weightlifting and keeping in shape. You'll have to watch it, Watson, or you'll put some flab on that flat waistline if you're right there where the food is!"

The guy was being nice to me! He was even half-kidding me!

Some men came in from the outside for a weightlifting tournament where I was one of the lifters. One of the men, who was as big as me and a good weightlifter, got to watching me and started talking to me.

"My name is Ron Ragland," he said, coming up to talk to me.

"Frank Watson," I said. In prison you sometimes forget that there are good people out there and that they have nice manners.

"Frank, have you heard about the Community Volunteers program?"

"Don't believe I have."

"Well, it's set up by the North Carolina Department of Corrections to get people outside the walls interested in the welfare of prisoners and also to get the general public informed about prison life. It's one of Mr. Bounds's projects."

The-hell-you-say, I muttered to myself.

146

"You and I are somewhat alike in our interests, and I'd like to work out with you now and then, see if you can teach me some tricks. Is that O.K. with you?"

"Sure."

Some months after that I was in the kitchen deep-frying chicken for supper. I'd washed pots and pans for the first month there, and then they'd moved me up.

"Sergeant wants to see you, Watson."

"Oh hell, what'd I do now? I'm busy."

"Don't ask me. Down at the desk in the back hall, control center."

So I took off my apron, washed my hands, told another cook to take over and went.

"I hear you want to see me, Sergeant. What'd I do?"

"Got yourself a small opportunity, Watson. There's a school teacher waiting to see you."

"*School teacher?* I ain't about to go to no damn *school!* I'm one of those old dogs that can't learn no new tricks."

"Try it. Nobody ever said you was *dumb*, Watson. Check him out."

"Oh, it's a man. Well, that's a little better."

Waiting in the office was Charles E. Wheeler, a professor of Criminology for Florida State University in Tallahassee—I didn't tell him about my big trip to Tallahassee until a long time later—and Sergeant Raeford Tart, whom I already knew. Wheeler was the first professor of anything I ever met. Damn nice guy, easy to talk to. Looked like a professor, of course, kind of quiet, with glasses, about six feet but not heavy.

"Mr. Watson, we have some money from the Federal government to try out Mr. Bounds's idea. It's to be a school to train prisoners as social workers."

"Why me? I ain't very social!"

He laughed. "That's exactly why. Our theory is that since

no one else can handle incorrigibles, maybe other incorrigibles can do the job. We feel we can hardly lose because we haven't been doing very well by any other method."

"Incorrigible? That's one of the words they call me. There are a whole lot of other ones if you have time to listen."

"I know about them," he said. "Now, our idea is to select some really hard-core men from all the units of the State and give them four courses: Counseling, Abnormal Psychology, Sociology, and Correctional Administration. It's a nine month training program. You'll have class work and supervised practical experience, doing counseling with the same men who are with you on H Block, your cell mates."

The sergeant grabbed a paper towel and handed it to me. I was plenty glad to have something to wipe my eyes with, I was laughing so hard, just another gimmick of the prison system.

Wheeler didn't seem to notice. "The plan has a fancy title, Group Educational Training Program, and Mr. Bounds wants us to give it a special name, sort of symbolizing what we have in mind. New Careers, he's calling it."

"Mr. Bounds? The top man? *Him?*"

"Him! Whose side do you think he's on, Mr. Watson? In case you don't know, he's employed by the State, but he's on the side of the men in here, whenever he can be. He's one of our top penologists. That's why we decided to work here."

"I suppose I'll have to think about it," I said, sitting there like a lump.

"How long will that take, Mr. Watson?"

"Till about now. If you ain't puttin' me on—when do we start?"

One of the things I didn't like about it, after I got settled down enough to try to think it through, was that we trainees were to be put on E Block, which is also on the West End along with H Block. I'd just gotten myself off the West End for good behavior. Rocks in their heads, that's what they had.

"There is a good reason for this, Mr. Watson. You don't want the other inmates to think you're something special, like these do-gooders that come in from the outside and think they can change the world without knowing what the world is like. Several of the hard-core men we had selected turned us down because they were afraid of damaging their image as tough guys. Did you know that?"

"What image? What good does it do 'em?"

"Glad to hear you say that. So, you will be celled with, and go to school with, the same men you've been doing time with all these years. When you make honor grade, you can move to the North Central Correctional Center, and we'll begin your training. This is a pilot program, you know. We've picked six men to start. Are you game?"

"Damn right! I ain't got nothin' to lose." I looked out the window at those gray walls and iron fences. The old hate came boiling up in my throat. That prison is over a hundred years old. Plenty had happened there in that century, executions, murders, horror of every kind, but nothing like this. I used to think that ideas of handling prisoners hadn't changed in a hundred years either. Punish, punish, punish. Kill their manhood; make 'em into savages, vicious animals; don't trust 'em with anything; beat 'em down so their minds disappear and they don't give you any more trouble. I used to think I'd die in prison, as thousands of men do, and never get to see a woods or a small child or even a bird again.

Wheeler was still talking, ". . . pilot group, succeed or fail, it's up to you. We got the six worst, frankly, at least by their records, but men with high intelligence, leadership qualities, reliability, trustworthiness, even though their trustworthiness had a wrong focus. I hear it from prisoners and guards and officials that when Frank Watson gives his word, he'll stick by it."

"My granddaddy was a Baptist preacher."

"That doesn't always do it, Mr. Watson. In your case it might have helped and might not. We found out you're not an informer, and when you make up your mind about something, even if it's tearing up a maximum security prison, heaven and earth can't stop you. I guess that's supposed to be a compliment."

I just looked at him.

"You'll be getting knocked down some more, plenty more," he said soberly. "This deal isn't going to sit well with the other inmates, and I'm sure some of the administration people will work hard to scuttle it, but we'll try." He shook my hand. The sergeant almost had to lead me out the door. Frank Watson, Incorrigible, Outlaw, shaking hands with a college professor. And starting to *school.*

Frank Watson, hard-core con, was at a loss for words.

There hadn't been many red letter days in my life, not good ones, but the day I made honor grade and got moved to the North Central Correctional Unit to start my training was as bright as the sun.

We were given a case load of twelve prisoners from H Block to interview, counsel, test, and evaluate, using tape recorders and playing the tapes back in class. That way we could study techniques and make suggestions for each other. We interviewed prison officials from lieutenants to the warden to the commissioner. Of course, we all had our hang-ups, so that's why we worked in our round table discussions with our instructors. It wasn't easy. Sometimes it was pretty much like our H Block bull sessions, and we really lit into each other.

The academic classes meant a great deal of reading and

book-larnin', but I'd been reading ever since I could spell out the words. In our bull sessions they made us work on our speech too. We'd have to meet parents, officials, well-educated people at all levels.

On top of all the other tough things that were thrown at us, the old-time correctional officers were fighting tooth and nail to undermine the program. They didn't believe that a man in prison could possibly change for the better. They'd put all kinds of obstacles in our way and harass us underhandedly, hoping we'd fail so they'd be right.

"Remember, men," Wheeler would caution us, "we warned you. That's why we picked the toughest, hardest men we could find in the whole system. We knew you'd have to fight everything—yourselves, other prisoners, officials, even the public. Can you stick to your guns?"

"*Yeah!*"

A couple of times Charlie—that's Mr. Wheeler, but we were all calling him Charlie by then—gave me a few private tips. "Frank, you're sort of the king-pin in this operation. If you quit, we'll fail. It's as simple as that. Some of the hard-liner guards keep telling me you're the least likely to succeed. How do you feel about it?"

"Did any of those cats tell you I was a quitter?"

"Quite the contrary! Some of them seemed to wish you had been!"

"Well, I ain't—I'm not going to quit now. Trust me!"

One did fail, but the other five of us saw it through for the nine months. We were the first group. That kind of put extra pressure on us to make it.

There had been talk all along that we would be paroled and hired by the North Carolina Department of Corrections as counselors, the units and destinations to be determined by Commissioner Bounds.

"We're gonna join the *enemy!* We're switchin' sides!" We got so we could laugh about working for the Establishment and especially about our own unbelievable chance to have a New Career. We'd be employed, hired, *paid*, by the very men we had hated.

In the first fifty years of my life, what did I respect? Not much of anything. Not myself. I respected, let's see, a strong body, a good gun with plenty of ammunition, a knife, a decent woman—but I didn't know very many—and what else? Cedar Arm Tucker was the first man I could admire; then all of a sudden there was Ron Ragland, Charlie Wheeler, and Lee Bounds—he had great ideas in prison reform and at the same time a deep respect for the law. We began to see it too, through him.

When my first half-century of life was over, I finally knew where I was going. And a little bit of how to get there.

19

VALENTINE'S DAY, 1972. FRANK WATSON, PAROLEE, ALMOST-FREE man, had never been so nervous in his whole life. I was getting out after sixteen years of being locked up. It was the wildest kind of dream realized, but I wasn't just getting sprung into some non-prison paradise; I was going to have to try working with, instead of against, the system I'd been fighting since I was about ten years old. I was not only joining the enemy on their territory, I'd be smack in the middle of them, trying to think and act the way they did.

My head is a very stubborn one, but I'd had nine months of bending and twisting and pushing and pounding on it, trying to get it set a little straighter. Maybe nine months wouldn't hold up against forty years, but I was stubborn enough to try.

The first thing, like every job I ever did, was to get a car. This one had to be legit! *I'd never owned one.* Charlie talked it over with his wife, and she agreed that they would cosign a $1,200 loan for me for a second-hand 1968 Cougar I'd found. When I look back, I can hardly imagine how much guts they had, to trust me that much!

Charlie went with me to the bank. Imagine, walking in the front door of a *bank*, on a business day, unarmed, and not on the lookout for a cop! The loan officer looked up.

"Now, Mr. Watson, if you'll just fill out this application, we'll try to process your loan as quickly as we can." He pushed a paper in front of me and pointed to the line on Previous Employment.

I looked at Charlie and Charlie looked at me.

"Play it straight, Frank."

So I wrote down that I had been in prison. The guy looked at it, and his eyebrows flew up, then down, then up, then down as he put on his banker's face and asked me what the charge had been. I looked at Charlie again.

"Armed robbery."

"Well—" I could see him looking around for a uniformed guard or a dangling pair of handcuffs.

"It's O.K.," Charlie said. "I'll vouch for him."

All of a sudden I was an average citizen, the kind who owes money at the bank and has a job and drives a mortgaged car. I got into the Cougar as if I'd been driving for a living, but I hadn't had my hands on a wheel for sixteen years. I literally flew along in it, much too fast. If I could sing, I'd have been doing some fancy hollering as I drove out to Polk Youth Center, west of Raleigh. I'd never gone for a *job* interview before. I'd had plenty of the other kind.

I sat there nervously talking to Mr. R. E. Jones, the Superintendent, with my thoughts going in a thousand directions. One part of me wanted to do anything I possibly could for the young guys coming in there, just starting out on the road I'd taken so disastrously when I was their age. If anyone could tell it like it is, it would be me. The other part of me rebelled against going through those gates and fences with their bristly armed guards. Would they ever entirely trust me as a State employee? I'd gone to school to learn my job, but going to school wasn't at all the same as actually working in the system. Policy, procedure, protocol, how did it all work? I heard myself answering Mr. Jones, "I can tell you this, sir, I'm the kind of guy that finishes any job he starts."

"So I hear," he said with a very small smile. "This job will be quite different from any you've—well, any you've taken on before, Mr. Watson."

"I know, sir, but I'll do my best."

By the third day I got to thinking about finding a broad. I'd been thinking about it for sixteen years, but I'd been too busy to get to it at first. I'd even had to sign up for Social Security and income tax deductions—this business of being a "civilian" might not be so good after all.

I spent the biggest part of Friday night sniffing around for a piece of ass like an old hound looking for something to screw. I found one, what you might call a fireball.

When we went to bed on Friday night, I weighed 225 pounds. When we came out on Monday, I was down to 195. No, we didn't eat. Just took time out for bathroom trips now and then. I didn't see the girl again for a month.

On Monday morning, starting my new job, I staggered in, trim in the waistline and weak in the knees. I looked around me with a wary eye. Staff, Frank, you're *staff* now, I kept saying to myself. Don't blow it. Remember the gate opened for you to come in. It will open for you to go out. No sweat. But I was on the spot, with the officials, other staff people, and *me*.

"Mr. Watson, if you were going to escape from Polk, how would you do it? You seem to know all kinds of secrets." I still hear that ten times a day, especially from the newer ones.

"I wouldn't! No secrets. I just wouldn't. I'd take my licks, I'd grab every chance they give me to learn some kind of trade or skill, and man, I'd amount to something. I wasted fifty years and thousands of dollars finding that out."

Some of them laugh, some of them listen and ask me more questions; some of their parents are stunned to find out who I am and what I was before. All I say is: *You can change. I did.*

The first day they gave me a hard time about what I would wear. I looked pretty damn sharp in new double-knit slacks, black chukka-type shoes with buckles, and a sport shirt, hair trimmed, nails clean. I hate the hippie stuff.

"Mr. Watson, the staff people always wear shirt-and-tie. I'd suggest that you do the same. We have to look professional, you know."

The old Cherokee—or maybe it really was Apache—began to rise. I tried to smile. "No way!" I said. "For one thing, a necktie to me means a *rope*. I don't want that, ever!" Of course they laughed, kind of self-consciously. Then I said, "To be serious, if I look too 'professional,' I'm not going to get to first base with these young fellows. I always keep myself clean, you know that, but if I show up here in a shirt and tie like a cop in civvies, they'll really turn off. I won't get to first base with them. I've got to get next to them as fast as I can—right?—and the way I look is plenty important. Trust me. O.K.? I know what I'm talking about."

Finally they said all right, we'd try it. Now some of them dress casually too, especially if they don't work in the front office. We've got enough going against us, God knows. If I could spare just one kid all, or any, of the licks I've had, I'd wear a space suit or a kitchen apron or a pink bath towel, but it isn't that easy. The *boys* are what matter to me, any way I can reach them.

When I went to work as a Counselor in a prison camp, I had conflicting thoughts, believe me. One side of me was happy as a hound dog to be free again, even if my freedom was under the supervision of both the State and Federal governments. The other side of me kept saying cop-out, cop-out, turncoat, joining-the-enemy, you're just a *traitor*. Here I was working for, and getting paid by, the very people I'd spent half my life hating, fighting, despising. *Cop-out!* You're throwing in the towel, Watson! You're a *quitter*.

It took me a year to get over that feeling.

At my job interview at Polk Youth Center, I didn't like what I saw. Locked gates, uniforms, cells, barbed-wire fences, guard towers. Prison, that's what it was. Prison! And I was going right back into it. But there was a difference: I could get out. So I sat down and talked turkey to myself. *Frank Watson, you're a fighter. A hell of a good one. You ain't used to gettin' licked. Well? You gonna let 'em whip you this time? Whose fault will it be?*

Then I remembered that when I was getting myself in shape for some big Pro fight, I'd allow myself six months of weight-lifting, jogging, sparring, push-ups, and I'd win. Now I'd had *nine* months of heavyweight brain stuff and a stack of trainers, twice as many as I'd ever had before, all pulling for me. Would I lose the battle? Yeah, I might. Why not be honest? I've always been honest.

During that long training period, I had already told myself that I'd never go back to prison, never, unless someone bad-rapped me for something I didn't do. Sure, I hated the law, but I knew better than most people that there are very few innocent people behind bars. Maybe one to thousands of the guilty ones. It's just that you hear about the innocent ones. And I do know that we have to have prisons. No other way.

What really worried me more than any problem with myself was the attitude of other staff members. Maybe they wouldn't accept me as a fellow-employee of the State of North Carolina, having been one of its prize Bad Boys for so long. I felt that I was intelligent enough to handle my job—that didn't bother me too much—but what if the other men wouldn't cooperate with me on the programs and custodial work?

Were there rat-finks on the outside too? Well, I'd never quit on anything before, so I'd soon find out.

In September, 1971, during our training program, there was that terrible prison riot at Attica, New York, where all those men were killed. When I read about that and thought about how it might have been prevented if the inmates had had counseling by guys who knew the ropes, I figured that I was

157

doing the right thing. I had a lot of friends in prison and still do; maybe I could help a couple of them or keep some kids from going that route.

I wasn't going to be one of those damn do-gooders. I'd be the guy who could tell it like it is, because I can; but I'd also be the guy they could talk to so they'd have someone listening to their side of the story.

They were going to give me the really wild ones that came in, figuring I knew the very worst of life both in and out of the slammer. Everybody knows that young guys going into prison for the first time, no matter what they did, are getting into a graduate school of crime and will come out a hundred times worse than when they went in. All I needed to do was to look back over twenty-seven years.

It didn't take long for word from the grapevine to get to me: *Frank Watson isn't going to succeed.* How could a guy fifty years old change his attitude toward prison, authority, crime, law enforcement, and life in general? The newspapers picked up my story, of course, and that didn't help with the other employees.

The Durham *Morning Herald*, March 11, 1972

An ex-convict who once was hunted as an outlaw is playing a key role in an inmate counseling program that officials think could be the safety valve to spare North Carolina prisons another riot such as the one in 1968.

Frank Watson of Asheville, paroled last month after serving sentences for armed robbery, escape and safecracking, is one of five ex-convicts qualifying as counselors for the North Carolina Department of Corrections. . . . "And he's doing a heck of a good job," said Robert Jones, superintendent of the 420-inmate center.

During all my years as a prisoner, I had kept myself going by one saying: *They can kill me, but they can't beat me.* I was still saying the same thing and about the same kind of people, but now I was one of them. *Wow.*

20

ONE OF THE STRANGEST THINGS THAT STARTED HAPPENING TO me right away was that people invited me to social affairs! I went, and enjoyed them! Along in March there was to be an afternoon picnic at Pullen Park, a big city park halfway between the University, where I had taken my training, and Central Prison, where I had taken my punishment.

A prisoner friend of mine had fixed up a blind date for me, but the girl's car broke down and she couldn't make it. His wife asked a neighbor of hers if she would like to go. At first she thought she would because she was divorced and very lonely, but when she found out who her date was, she remembered all that stuff in the papers about me and got scared off. She had a four-year-old son and more trouble than she could manage already. Her husband had left her with nothing but a small baby, and she'd had it plenty rough. All she needed was to get tangled up with an ex-con.

Nothing might have come of it if her little boy, David, hadn't heard the conversation with the neighbor and set up a howl about missing a picnic. She finally said well, yes, she guessed she'd go. Sundays were even lonelier than the rest of the week, and David did need an outing.

I married her one month later, April 29, 1972.

Our wedding at Charlie Wheeler's house had just a few guests. The ceremony was performed by the chaplain from the prison. Carolyn looked so sweet and fragile; I wanted to take care of her forever. She's tiny and quiet, half my size. She wore a dress with a long blue paisley skirt and a white

159

top. Charlie's wife had made a bouquet for her from the wild-flowers nearby and a boutonniere for me. Frank Watson, Incorrigible, wearing a flower! And being a sentimental fool about it!

There were white wedding bells hanging from the ceiling lamps, and on the table were all kinds of party foods that Mrs. Wheeler had made, a big bowl of punch, cookies, nuts, mints. Everything looked as if it should have had its picture in a magazine.

I got to laughing in the middle of the service, I was so embarrassed. Carolyn couldn't get my wedding ring on over the big knuckles in my finger. It fitted all right at the jewelry store, but I guess I was nervous or something. It's on now. To stay.

We opened our gifts—I still can't get used to the idea of someone giving me a present—went to the Seashore Restaurant for supper, got some records from her sister and went to our rented trailer to begin our life together.

At my job the hardest thing to learn was to follow policy and procedure. How to manage the stacks of paperwork—this still bugs me, where to go to get the proper answer, what move to make when you struck a roadblock in the chain of command. Finally I learned that you start at the bottom and follow the chain up to wherever you find out what you wanted to know. Taking matters into my own hands and knocking a few heads together or shooting up the place wouldn't work any more!

My days start about 8:00 A.M. and go until 5:00 or 5:30; then each Counselor spends one evening a week, sometimes more, just circulating wherever the boys are so they can talk to us. We walk around the compound, the dormitories, the academic and vocational sections, down to Segregation, "the

160

hole," anyplace. The door to my office is always open unless I'm in a conference that shouldn't be interrupted. The boys know they can talk to me any time, unless I'm tied up with something that can't be put off, like a Staff meeting, Honor-Grade Committee hearing, or the Disciplinary Board. Funny how important it is to these kids just to have someone to listen. Some of their gripes may seem pretty small to someone else, but to the kid they're mighty big problems.

It took a long time for me to get used to being part of the System I'd been cussing out and fighting most of my life, but every time I have to make a decision now it gets easier because I'm on the right path. I'm sure of it. Of course we have to have laws and prisons, but when I see a boy maybe eighteen years old, already in deep trouble and heading for worse, I ask myself what caused him to take this course? How can we turn him around?

What turned *me* around? *Not prison.* Not prison, but people. People like Lee Bounds, Charlie Wheeler, Ron Ragland, Cedar Arm Tucker, my fine son, Sam Garrison, now the warden at Central Prison, Randy Monchick, who was Wheeler's assistant in the New Careers program, and a half dozen others who believed in me and gave me a chance. And hope. If you don't have hope, you're gone.

What good did all that punishment do me? All those threats? Those *years* in the hole? That starvation? That hanging on the wall for nearly three days with my feet not touching the floor? That steady humiliation and degradation? *None.* Nothing turned me around until I got a chance to be a useful human being through the right kind of rehabilitation and faith in the possibilities. I can hardly describe what it means to be *trusted.*

Twenty-seven years of total failure by the whole prison system, even Alcatraz and Ivy Bluff. Prisons shouldn't be fancy

161

hotels, of course, but prisoners are people. And we do have to live with politics one way or another—that's a fact of life—but there won't be any improvement in prison rehabilitation programs until politics gets out of the prison system and they stop thinking only of punishment. Handling guys like me, who won't knuckle down to their rules, and a lot of men even worse, takes Pros. I think they call them penologists. Men who know prisoners as well as prisons. There's a standing joke in the lower echelons that today's janitor may be tomorrow's administrator and consequently your boss, so watch it!

I guess the reason I'm popping off about this is that the program which really gave me back my life after I'd been trying to throw it away was canceled when the first money ran out. There were two nine-month training programs and one six-month one, and that was it. Not all the men who had the chance made it, I know, but they did have a chance and all of them were chosen from the very worst of the lot. For some reason it makes me think of that story of The Lost Sheep. About thirty men went through this schooling.

Well, back to the good things. While I was trying to get myself geared to work into the system and do as good a job as I could, in June, Carolyn told me that we were going to have a baby. I was so happy I was just about jumping.

In some of those long, secret prayer-talks I had with God, I had promised Him that if I ever had a family again I would cherish it forever. I'd be a real father, a man the kid could be proud of. Funny, I was finding out that God was listening. When I was my old criminal self, I'd ask Him to help get me through a robbery without hurting anyone or getting myself killed or to help me hide someplace until the cops left—big as I am I'm hard to hide!—then I'd think that when I was safe, God was on my side. I'd look up and say, "Thank you, Lord!

Thank you!" And when something went wrong, I'd think His back was turned. Yeah, I was plenty mixed up.

When I knew there would be another child in our household, I asked Carolyn, "Do you think I should adopt David? Then he'd be mine too, and wear my name. Be honest with me. How do you feel?"

Her face really lit up. "If you want to. It's your decision. You're already his father in every way but birth."

"I'll check it out." Well, by that time I was beginning to think I could move mountains in this new life of mine, but I found out that an ex-con isn't considered any great bargain as an adoptive parent. We went ahead anyway, hired a lawyer to process the papers and handle all the red tape. It took eight months, but at the end of that time David's name became Watson.

His little brother, Roy Lane Watson, was born at four o'clock in the morning on February 28, 1973, a little more than a year after his papa got out of the slammer. We named him for Carolyn's father. So I had three sons, one adopted, two others twenty-seven years apart. And man, am I proud of that older one! He came to see me even before I got out of prison, and I've seen him a couple of times since. Taller than me, handsome, decent as they come, good job, two kids about the ages of my little ones, one of his a girl, first girl in the Watson family since the Year One. Betty Sue did a great job of raising him by herself.

I never did tell him that the first thing that started me in a new direction was when she brought him to see me when he was a teen-ager. Sounds too much like soap opera.

When Roy Lane was two days old, they dressed me up in a hospital gown—they don't have many in size 52—and put him in my arms. I could have held all of him in one hand. He was so strong that he was already trying to hold his head up. His fist was the size of my thumb. His little tongue ran in and out like a pet mouse.

"I guess I don't look like no madonna," I said, trying to make a joke so I wouldn't sniffle.

In spite of all that happiness, a couple of months later the old Cherokee fire got into me, and I managed to forget all those promises to God and Carolyn and myself. I don't even remember what the fuss was about, but I decided to leave home. I spent half the night loading all my stuff into the Cougar, in and out of the house until the car was jam-packed. When I went back to make sure I hadn't forgotten anything, we began to talk, not saying much at first, then letting it all hang out until we got the whole hassle settled.

So, I spent the rest of the night *unloading* everything and putting it back where it belonged. Carolyn, just as stubborn as me, which is pretty damn stubborn, stood by the door and watched me. Didn't make a move or say a word. Just watched.

"You didn't lift a finger to help me!"

"It wasn't my stuff."

If I had been the old me, I'd have whacked her one. Now we laugh about it, but that night it wasn't funny. Not a damn bit funny.

At first my job was to get acquainted with the inmates at Polk Youth Center (as well as to learn to work with the system), to try to get the boys' respect and confidence and perhaps to gain a bit more for myself. That first year was hell because the hardest nut to crack was Frank Watson, to get him to realize that he was a person of value. When that was done, he could start working with the inmates on the same score for themselves. You are a *person*, you have *value*. I'd never heard that kind of talk in prison.

There are some plenty frightening characters that come into

164

this Center. A few of them are from the "best families," with big cars, college educations, expensive clothes, well-known names, but most are from the poorer classes of people. Some have already committed two murders and they're not yet twenty. All I had done at that age was to get into fights and steal some food from a mailbox.

No, I never killed anyone and hope I never have to. If you take a person's life, it's gone. Money he can get back. And I knew, too, that the government was pretty strict about enforcing the death penalty, so I figured that if I took a life I'd lose my own.

Some of these boys are already farther down the hill than I ever was. I've smashed up a lot of people, but only finks, screws, and guys trying to kill me first. I never did hurt the people I was robbing, except one time I broke a fellow's wrist. I thought of myself as a gentleman robber, something like Robin Hood, although I wasn't much at giving the loot to the poor. I scared hell out of 'em, I know that, but I never really used weapons except on scum that got in my way. If you're a real Pro, I always told myself, you're going to win and you don't have to hurt your victim. Oh, maybe in his pocketbook, but no place else.

I must sound like one of those Pharisee fellows.

One of our biggest problems now is drugs. It's so bad that we have to have a special drug counselor. Drugs have always been a part of life on the streets, but I never got into them. Now it seems to be the "in" thing for guys that have everything. Their parents drive up in Cadillacs, Lincolns, dressed fit to kill and bringing their pore li'l ole boy lots of special goodies.

Hell, instead of special goodies brought in to him, he should have had his ass kicked long ago. *And so should Mom and Pop.*

We used to have a lot of race trouble here too, but I'd get

hold of the ringleaders, especially the black ones, and lay it on the line. "Stop trying to shift blame from yourself! Stop using the excuse of being black! I don't give a hootin' damn what color you are, or anyone else is. What you have got to do is to figure out the difference between *right* and *wrong*, not the difference between black skin and white skin. When you're right, I'm your friend, but I'm never your patsy. Now start gettin' your head together. And let me take care of those weapons of yours for a while. All of 'em: knives, clubs, guns."

You think I never knew the difference between right and wrong, doing all that stuff I did? Of course I knew. But I just told myself that no one gave a damn what crap I got tangled up with, and no one ever gave me credit for what I did right —I guess they didn't get many chances. I'd get caught; then I'd say, "Well, I don't have nothin' else to do, so I might as well sit in the lockup for a while, put in the time." And, of course, start scheming about escaping, getting smarter than the screws, beating them at their own game. Twelve times I escaped. Am I proud of it? Hell, no! Not any longer. I'm ashamed. Disgusted.

The New Testament says you should have a new bottle for new wine—I can't quite manage that, past fifty already—but I can be a new man inside this old one.

Do I believe in miracles? *Hell, Yes!* I am one.

Epilogue

AFTER I HAD MY SPECIAL TRAINING, GOT OUT OF CENTRAL PRISON, started on my new job, and married Carolyn, my life went in a new direction. By June, 1975, I was off all parole, State and Federal, a totally free man for the first time in nearly thirty-five years.

I've been promoted and given commendations, and I'm busier than I ever dreamed I could be. In prison you aren't really busy, even on the rock hole. You're just putting in time, slaving your tail off and hating everyone. I'm now (1976) Program Supervisor for Polk Youth Center, where we have over five hundred young guys in trouble, most of them eighteen to twenty-one years of age. My work must be O.K. because I keep getting awards: The Jaycee Presidential Award in 1974, Counselor of the Year and Coordinator of the Year for 1975, diplomas from workshops I've attended and special training sessions they send me to. Most amazing of all, I'm on the part-time staff of the Officers' Training School. Yes, I help show the prison guards what to look for while they are on duty. Who knows more about it than I do? Too bad I never got any diplomas for outwitting guards—we could paper a room with them. A big room.

This may sound sentimental, but sometimes I sit in my office up in one corner of this prison after things have quieted down and marvel at what has happened to me: a man who has been to Hell, every corner of it, and met the Devil so many times that most of my life was spent in his company. Now I'm compassionate towards people's problems. I never see color or crime or label. I see a *person*. To my mind this is what Rehabilitation really is: *To see people in trouble as persons*, and to *listen*. It sounds simple.

Rehabilitation is one of those words that get kicked around a lot. To some people it means programs, training, discipline, rewards for effort. Hell, that's the way you train animals! Too many people, who probably mean well, are trying to work at rehabilitating someone in trouble without having been there themselves. Education and theories are great, but they have to be combined with a big dose of good old horse sense and some first-hand experience, or they won't work. The old saying "It takes one to know one" could be "It takes one to help one." Charlie Wheeler's and Lee Bounds's philosophies, I guess. They had an uphill fight to get a chance even to try out this wild theory of using Incorrigibles to help Incorrigibles, but for me, as hard-core a criminal as they could find, it was a life-saver. Literally. I hope I've helped at least some of the dozens of boys who know me. There are still some men in prison who could make it too if they had the kind of help I had and were given half a chance. In turn, they could help other people. Pass it on, you might say.

It's a good thing they had us work on our speech and our grammar because I make so many talks to civic clubs, churches—Frank Watson talking to a whole roomful of dressed-up church ladies!—youth groups, college classes, and men's clubs. When half the audience have Ph.D.'s, Frank Watson is enough of a ham that he wants to hold his own. This is the old Cherokee *pride*, not the temper. Probably Grandpa Cook never thought of little Frankie as a missionary, but I guess that's what he is, fightin' the Devil and tryin' to wash his hands of sin.

What do I talk about? Mostly myself. My new life and what

a miracle it is at middle age. I sound off on the law too. *The criminal laws need to be changed.* Now the lawbreaker is the winner. That's the reason so many people who have been robbed, raped, assaulted, cheated, and attacked don't squawk. They know they can't win. I heard somewhere that the proportion of those who commit crimes and get punished is less than one in thirteen. *Any* punishment at all. And if you've got enough money, you can get out of anything. All you need to do is read the papers. Think back over the things that have happened in the seventies. In high places, or even low places. When there's enough money, you can get off.

I know both sides of the story. From the side of law and order, I say, *"Don't give the lawbreaker any rope. Be fair, treat him like a person, but make the law stick."* From the other side of the fence, I say, *"Take your punishment like a man."* Some of these boys at Polk think they can butter me up just because I show concern for them and listen to their troubles. They want me to get them off light. *"No way,"* I tell them. *"No way. When you get your head on straight and are ready to work for something better in life than this road you're heading down, I'll help you. Not before. First you have to earn help by helping yourself."*

One word I use with them is *stupidity.* Going wrong is just plain stupid. I didn't always get a fair shake, but most of the time I did if I'd had the sense to know it and to use it. Some people outside the walls are saying that rehabilitation of prisoners won't work, isn't worth trying, is dangerous to society and all that hogwash. Nothing works if you don't want it to. A new life has to come from the inside. *Get off your ass!* Take whatever chance is offered to you and *make it work for you.*

One of the most effective groups working with youthful offenders is the Junior Chamber of Commerce, the Jaycees. They organize programs within prison units and see that each inmate has one man who is his friend, like a Big Brother. When the Blue Ridge Chapter first started in the prisons, there was a sensational incident, not at our unit, that did a great deal of damage. A young inmate was made president of the prison chapter and allowed out to make a speech to a civic club, under guard, of course. A public relations idea, I guess. He managed to escape, and before he was caught, he had committed a murder. There were headlines and shock waves all over the country. It gave the whole Jaycee program a black eye.

We really had to dig in then to get our own unit on its feet, to make membership an honor to be earned, and to help those boys who are "loners" learn to work in a group constructively. Only about ten per cent of the unit's population is allowed to belong, and a likely member has to wait until there is a vacancy. As far as I know there has never been another bad scene. I have taken boys on overnight trips and to State conventions and have never had one minute's trouble of any kind.

Among many other things, the Jaycees pay for boys to get special training so they can get decent jobs on the outside. They buy sports equipment, tapes, records. Their first big outside project was to adopt two foreign orphans through the Christian Children's Fund. They earn their money by carwashes inside the fence, cookouts where the public can buy hamburgers or barbecue at the gate, photography for visitors, Christmas cards, handmade candles. They're a busy bunch. And the local Jaycees who have helped sponsor them have a new insight into the needs and problems of young men in trouble.

The thing I hate to do is to go after escapees. I know too much about what can happen to a desperate kid on the run. We have some mighty desperate ones, believe me. When we get a boy back and calmed down a little, I try to find out what's eating him. "I got too many problems, Mr. Watson. You know what my dad did when I got caught dealing in drugs. And my mom—she panicked. And now my girl . . ."

"Is that the real story?" I ask. "Let's take a look at *you*. What's ahead? You're the only one who can decide. How'd you like it out there in the swamps, especially during that storm? Nearly freeze? Starve? Get snake-bit? Shot at? Did they send the dogs? You like being sniffed at by a bloodhound? Damn right I know how it is, *all of it*. I don't lie. Well, you decide. Start talkin'. I can listen all night if I have to."

Sometimes I do, if that's what he needs. After all, he's a human being, not just a prisoner. Who knows the difference better than Frank Watson? I've been there and back.